It Just So Happened

Supernatural Incidents
and
Timely Coincidents

Memoirs of life in the Middle East

David Holmes

ISBN: 978-1-916820-69-2

itjustsohappened@yahoo.com

CONTENTS

Introduction

Lord, you establish peace for us; all that we have accomplished you have done for us,… but your name alone do we honour. Isaiah 26 v 12-13.

To condense twelve very full, excitingly active, years of life into some forty short stories is an impossibility. All these stories seek to do is to, firstly, give some small insight into the joys and difficulties of the life we led abroad and then secondly, and much more importantly, to show how we were upheld and encouraged by what we were sure was the leading, guiding and safe keeping of God during that particular period of our lives.

Since the events recounted in these stories took place, and particularly in the last few years, my wife Doreen and I have often thought that we should record, mainly for the benefit of our sons and their children, something about that time we had spent working in the Middle East in association with Middle East Christian Outreach.

After what we at first perceived and then recognised as a "call" from God to work in the Middle East our first approach was to make contact with the Lebanon Evangelical Mission (LEM). I had seen something of

1

their work some twelve years earlier on a visit to the Lebanon when a student. It turned out that as we explored this area of work and service the LEM were just at the point of merging with two other Christian groups working in the same areas. Together they went on to be known as Middle East Christian Outreach or MECO for short.

MECO was an evangelical, interdenominational and international group of Christians who brought their skills to work alongside Middle Eastern Christians and churches in many countries in the region as and when political and social circumstances permitted.

As I write it occurs to me that I joined MECO as it was formed. Then some 42 years later, as a Trustee of MECO (UK), I was one of the trustees who helped oversee it merging with Serving In Mission (SIM).

In 1977 Doreen, I and our three boys, aged seven, five and nine months left England. We then lived in the capital city of Jordan, Amman until 1979 in order to begin to learn the Arabic language and to immerse ourselves in the culture of the Middle East. A move to Lebanon followed. There we lived in the mountain town of Brummana. Every day I travelled down the mountain into Beirut to teach in a school in the Christian area of East Beirut called Ashrafieh.

We returned to England in 1981 for what was scheduled to be one year but our return to Lebanon was delayed a few weeks due the Israeli invasion of the country that took place while we were away. A further year was then spent in Lebanon before we moved to Cyprus in 1983. For the next six years Larnaca, Cyprus acted as a base for the Media (video) work that we started. During this time Egypt was the country most visited by me in furthering the video work and this is reflected in the stories told.

During all this time we were both active in a local church with Doreen playing a major role in children's work in Lebanon along with ministry among ladies. This continued in Cyprus along with often providing hospitality and refreshment for a large number of people passing through Cyprus to and from many countries in the Middle East.

Today we live in a world where it is possible to have almost instant contact with anybody, anywhere in the world at any time we wish using mobile phones or one of the internet based applications in use today. At the time the events recounted took place the internet was unheard of and consequently email, Facebook, WhatsApp and Zoom were things of the future.

I, as the actual writer of most of the stories, am very conscious that the personal pronoun appears very frequently in the text but my wife Doreen is an integral part of that "I". Without her companionship, partnership and Godly wisdom none of what is described would have occurred. The very nature of the narrative makes it impossible to dispense with the "I" and "we" but it is our deepest wish and desire that people see past them and see the loving, caring hand of God shining through in many of the situations that our family faced.

Along with the missionary apostle Paul we believe that *"In him (God) we live and move and have our being"* (Acts 17 v 28) and also the truth of God's promise - *"Never will I leave you; never will I forsake you". So we say with confidence, "The Lord is my helper; I will not be afraid. What can man do to me?"* (Hebrews 13 v 5, 6).

While we believe that the Lord is indeed in control of our lives we are also aware that we have a free will, we have choices and sometimes difficult decisions to make when it may seem that we are "on our own".

As you read the stories that follow the statement "It just so happened" occurs in many of them. Then too, at the conclusion of many stories, a question is posed basically asking – **Did it just so happen? Did God supernaturally intervene in the circumstances described or was it just a timely, welcome coincident?**

I leave you, the reader, to ponder and decide.

1

The Journey Begins – Leaving England

The first time we travelled to Lebanon we were required to go via Cyprus as that was where the MECO headquarters were located and where our initial overseas briefing was to be completed. At that time Doreen's parents lived in Cyprus, where her father, seconded to the British Forces, worked in the meteorological office on a British air force base. Although a civilian he had the status of a British military officer and as such was able to purchase tickets on ordinary civilian flights to Cyprus at a much reduced rate for family members. So because of the greatly reduced cost we naturally bought our air tickets through him. On the hand written tickets was the travel class designation "FF" - short for Forces Fare.

When our family of five came to check in at London Heathrow airport we did so with some trepidation because we had so much luggage to take with us. Our permitted baggage allowance was grossly exceeded. This was not surprising as we were moving home from England to Jordan. At the check in desk I remarked to the woman that there were five of us checking in with "quite a lot of luggage". She took a look at our tickets and, pointing to another desk some distance away, said

"Oh – you should have checked in over there". Then after a slight hesitation as she looked at all our luggage went on to say "but don't worry I can do it here if you like." She proceeded to check through all our vastly overweight luggage with, to our surprise, not a mention of an excess baggage payment needing to be paid. She then told us that as the flight was delayed for two hours vouchers for purchasing breakfast were being provided. Then off she went to the check in counter she had earlier pointed to and returned with a handful of breakfast vouchers for us. We could not believe the monetary value that the vouchers added up too. Not only did they feed our family of five with a full English breakfast each but also my parents and another couple who had come to pray us on our way.

At the appointed time we said our goodbyes to my parents and friends and made our way to the airport "Gate" for departure. Once at the "Gate" we were picked out of the waiting crowd and shepherded to be the first to board the aircraft. We thought they did this because we had three young boys in tow! As we were ushered to our seats the air hostess apologised profusely that this particular aircraft only had economy class seats but that they had allocated us, what they thought, were the best seats with the most legroom and space at the front of the aircraft. Throughout the five hour flight we, and especially our three children, were very well looked after. It then gradually began to dawn on us the reason for this unexpected "special" treatment we were receiving – we guessed that it just so happened that the woman at the check in desk had mistakenly read the handwritten "FF" designation on our tickets to mean First Class Fare. At that time the baggage allowance for first class travel was very much greater than for ordinary economy tickets and so, we surmised, the reason why there was no question of us paying for our excess luggage. It also explained why our breakfast vouchers were so great in value and why they put us in what they considered the best seats on the airplane.

A supernatural incident or just a welcome coincident?

2

Moving Home to the Hashemite Kingdom of Jordan

Moving home is hard. Moving home to another country is harder. Moving home to another country with three young children is even harder! After many difficult decisions were made as to what should move with us we then had to decide what should travel with us by air and what should travel separately by ship. The possibility of air freighting all our belongings from England to Jordan was a non-starter as it would have been prohibitively expensive – something our budget just did not run to. Even the cost of sea freighting would be an expensive proposition.

Shortly after it became known that we were moving to the Middle East a friend phoned to see what our projected move entailed and how it was progressing. He then went on to ask "Do you know what my job is?" "I know you work for……." and named the large specialist metal production company in town. "That's right" he replied, "but do you know what my job is there?" I had to admit that I had no idea. "I'm the freight manager and despatch freight all over the world by air and sea every day. I'll arrange all the shipping for you if you like." He went on to say that because what we had to send was miniscule in both size and weight compared to his company's shipments when added to one of them the pro rata cost to us would also be miniscule compared to what we would have to pay if we arranged it ourselves. It just so happened that our friend was in the perfect occupation to help us and that also the company owner was quite happy to add our freight to theirs and charge us accordingly.

So it was that several weeks later I delivered to my friend's company freight yard two very large wooden boxes loaded with the belongings that were being sent to Jordan for us. We knew what ship they would be on, when it was leaving the dock in London and when it was expected to arrive in Jordan. It was due to arrive in the port of Aqaba in Jordan shortly after our own arrival. Our boxes would then be transported the 200 miles (325 km) to the importation and customs post that served Amman. We would then be notified that they were ready for collection.

While our freight was on the high seas our family travelled to Jordan by air, with a stop-over in Cyprus for a work briefing and a holiday. We found that not only did our sea freight travel at a greatly reduced cost but it also turned out that our grossly overweight air luggage travelled free of charge.

After we had been in Amman several weeks we got notification that our boxes were now ready for collection from the duty free freight and customs office compound just outside Amman. At that time a colleague, who had lived in the Middle East for some thirty years, was visiting us. She said that it was quite probable that I would not get all the paperwork and formalities needed to release our boxes done that day but to be prepared to have to complete the transaction the next day. If that happened she could accompany me the next day as she was fluent in Arabic.

I arrived at the customs compound early and quickly engaged a local "fixer" whose job it was to help and guide me through the process of releasing my goods. A multitude of documents and forms appeared that all needed dealing with, filling in and signing. My "fixer" certainly knew his way through and around the whole process and seemed to be "friends" with all the officials. Then, with a customs official at his side, he said "now we must find and open the boxes for inspection of the goods". It was the one thing I hoped might not happen but that everyone in Amman said would. The tops of both the boxes were very securely and strongly nailed down. It took another worker with a very large crowbar to prise open a corner of the first, smaller box. As the box was being opened the customs officer asked me what the contents were and if any of them were new items. I said that they were simply household items and children's toys from our home in England. He then turned his attention to the half opened box, put his hand in and felt around a bit and pulled out one of the children's toys. Turning to me he then asked how many children I had and was delighted when I said we had three boys – quite a prestigious thing in his culture. As the man with the crowbar turned his attention to the much larger box the customs officer stopped him with the words "no matter - enough - finish". With that the boxes were released to me to transport home.

Again with the help of my "fixer" a small truck was hired, loaded with my boxes and soon they were home and offloaded onto the waste land outside our front door. Our elderly lady visitor was incredulous when she knew I was back home so quickly with all our belongings intact. A record she said – both in time and cost.

Supernatural help or just coincidents?

3

Finding a New Flat

We had arrived in Amman, Jordan to find that the flat rented for us was not yet renovated or available to occupy as had been promised. Furthermore it was apparent that it would not be ready for our occupation for at least another three months.

So, after a week-long stay in a small dismal hotel, we moved into a minute semi-basement flat in the same building that our originally designated flat was to be found.

This temporary accommodation was very, very small and each evening we had to put a mattress down on the floor of the lounge for us to sleep on. With a few chairs squeezed beside the mattress it took up all the floor space and was a great embarrassment if any visitors came to the door as it was impossible to ask them in without them having to walk over the mattress!

During the daytime, sitting in the lounge, our eyes were level with the waste ground outside that was full of garbage and many a time we found that we were face to face with a rat, standing up on its hind legs, gazing in at us through the windows that, needless to say, we did not dare to open.

At that time, in Amman, there was a large influx of refugees from the civil war in Lebanon that made finding other, more suitable, accommodation all but impossible. So we looked forward to being able to move into our earmarked larger designated flat two floor above us and resigned ourselves to the necessary wait for it to be refurbished as promised especially as a whole year's advance rent had already been paid for it.

Finally with the so called refurbishment completed we found on viewing it that this flat had so many short-comings and problems about it that we felt that as a family of five we could not spend the next two years in such a place. What should we do? What could we do?

After much heart-searching we decided that we would have to tell our director in Cyprus that we simply had to find more suitable accommodation.

But as foreigners how could we find somewhere in the accommodation hungry capital city. As a start Doreen decided to immediately ask her language tutor if she knew of anywhere. However her tutor was unwell and so the visit for the lesson had to be postponed for a couple of days.

Two days later when asked, the tutor replied that it just so happened that a couple of flats had become available only the day before and were located across the road from our current semi-basement flat. They were on the top, fourth floor, of a new block of flats in the "compound" of the Assyrian Orthodox Church and school.

Straight away the tutor took Doreen, who collected me on the way, to see the Assyrian priest about the possibility of renting a place.

The priest got the surprise of his life when Doreen greeted him fluently in the Assyrian language - Doreen's heritage is Assyrian. The priest immediately took us up the ninety one stairs to view the newly completed flat. It was just perfect for us and the price was right.

To rent the property the priest said I would have to be interviewed and approved as a suitable person by the church committee. However he said that he would make sure they agreed to the let.

But what would our director say as it meant leaving the already paid for designated flat vacant and so would be a waste of mission money?

We returned to our flat to be met by a worried looking colleague who greeted us with the news that he faced the almost impossible job, as he saw it, of finding another flat in Amman for another couple due to arrive in Amman in just over a month's time.

What a relief. Two problems were already solved as the potentially vacant refurbished flat earmarked for us was well suited to the new people's needs. Furthermore we would not have the difficult situation of needing to refuse to move into what, for us, was unsuitable accommodation.

A supernatural incident or just a coincident?

4

Money at the Bank

The church committee followed the direction of their priest and agreed that we would be the tenants of their brand new apartment. A contract was duly signed but because money had to be transferred from a UK bank to the British Bank of the Middle East in Amman it was agreed that, as required, the full years rent would be paid ten days later giving ample time, so we thought, for the money to be transferred.

Ten days came and went and the colleague who held the bank account in his name kept reporting that the bank said that it had not yet received the money transfer. Grudgingly the church committee agreed to wait another week for the money – but definitely no longer they said. After, difficult to arrange, phone calls and telegrams to headquarters in Cyprus and our U.K. office we were assured that money had been transmitted to the bank in Amman and should have been with us during the past ten day period. Another week went by and we still awaited the arrival of the money in the bank account. We reached the day when the money had to be paid over that evening if we definitely wanted to secure the flat. So after language school had finished for the day I insisted that I also went to the bank with my colleague who I had no choice but to rely on because the bank account was only in his sole name. My name, by this time, should have been added to the account but for various reasons all the necessary paperwork had not yet been completed by the bank.

At the bank, again, we were informed by the cashier that there was not any money in the account to give us. The cashier's supervisor, when also questioned, said the same. The next stop was to insist, and it took much insistence, that we speak to the bank manager – a rather patronising British national as it turned out. Although we assured him that the money had left our UK account two and a half weeks before he simply said that if the cashiers and bank clerks said there was no money then that was the case and that there was nothing more he could or would do about it.

Finding it hard to believe the situation I found myself reluctant to leave the bank and the two of us simply started to walk around the bank foyer wondering what our next move should be. As we did this another cashier, who my colleague had dealt with on previous visits to the bank, beaconed us over and casually said "I think there is a lot of money that has come for your account". After all we had already been told by other cashiers, bank clerks and the manager we could hardly believe what we had just heard. We asked him to check for us and quickly he confirmed what we wished to hear. Naturally we then asked to draw the needed money out. "No problem", said the clerk, "I just need the passport of an account holder." But then a real problem came to light – my colleague had forgotten the fact that he needed his passport in order to access the account and had not brought it with him. The money was within our grasp but there was not time for us to go home, get the necessary passport and return to the bank before it closed for the day. Then, it just so happened that, a thought came into my mind that if, as we had wanted to do for some time, my name was added to the account could I then, using my name and passport (that I always carried with me) draw the money out today? "No problem", said the clerk once again. Twenty minutes later the paperwork was completed and the money was in my hands ready to be paid over to the Church committee that evening.

A few days later after a good clean of the flat, three days before Christmas, we moved into our new home.

A supernatural incident or a timely coincident?

5

Residence Permit

We had entered Jordan on visitor's visas and now the time had come to obtain a residence permit, for all five family members, or leave the country. It was a thing all foreigners dreaded as it always meant waiting in long queues and having to deal with complicated paperwork with usually little help from the officials processing the application.

On the designated day I made my way across town in search of the appropriate government office, located in the building that housed the dreaded secret police, where the permits were processed and issued. I duly arrived and as feared, although it was early in the morning, the office was packed with people. I was grateful to see that there were several, very orderly, queues leading to a number of processing counters. It soon became apparent that if anyone tried to jump a queue numerous police patrolling the room with batons in hands quickly and not a little gently moved them back to their original place or even right to the back of a queue once again. As the queue I joined had thirty to forty people in front of me I resigned myself to a long wait and, after seeing how slowly the line was moving,

I calculated that it would take four to five hours to simply get to the front of the queue.

Two officials sat working behind each counter but there was also a constant flow of police who came and went with paperwork given to them by those manning the counters. Then in the distance, it just so happened that, I thought I glimpsed someone in police uniform who I recognised.

Several minutes later a policeman suddenly appeared by my side and uttering one word, "come", took hold of my arm and guided me past all the waiting queues and placed me, apart from all of the waiting lines of people, near one of the processing counters. It seemed that I had been picked out for special treatment and that my residence application was going to be the next one to be dealt with. There were a few mutters of disapproval from some of the other waiting people but by this time I understood enough Arabic to understand that they were soon told to "be quiet" by the policemen patrolling the crowd. Behind the counters a girl in police uniform quietly nodded at me in recognition and then disappeared into a back office.

Very quickly, with great efficiency and an unusual amount of help, the paperwork for our family's five residence permits were processed and issued then and there as opposed to the applicant usually being required to return to the office to collect them a week later. While they were being processed the policewoman, without further indication of recognition, periodically appeared and spoke to the two officials dealing with our applications.

What, I had been warned, was likely to take all day or even longer was done and dusted in under two hours thanks to a certain policewoman being on duty in just the right place at the right time for me to benefit from being seen by her when I was standing at the back of a long queue of people.

Recently we had met a Jordanian young man in a local shop. He had told us that he was shortly going to study in America and we had talked a little and so it happened a few days later he came to visit us. This was not an unusual thing to happen particularly as I think he wanted to practice his English. He also observed the right protocol in that because, not only did he wish to talk to me but also to talk to Doreen as well, he needed to have a female companion with him. So he brought along his older sister who simply told us she worked in a government office – she did not mention she worked as a policewoman in the offices of the much feared secret police!

A supernatural incident or coincident?

6

The Butcher

Before we arrived in Jordan we were well aware that there would be many things that would be very different from what we were used to in the UK. One of the biggest differences was in the way we shopped and indeed in the shops themselves. The shop that was called a supermarket, found in the upmarket part of town, was only like a small "corner shop" in the UK – not even as big as a very, very small convenience store. In the more working class area where we lived the shops were all similar in shape and size to a small house garage and had roller metal shutters as their doors. They were stacked, top to bottom, with cardboard boxes full of goods in tins, glass jars, and plastic bottles and in individual cartons. Then there were also various "loose goods" such as rice, sugar, flour and many different dried pulses all stored in big sacks. We went shopping with a list of the things we required and the shopkeeper would retrieve each item from within the depths of the shop for us and where necessary dutifully weigh out the "loose goods" and put them in a paper bag. The cost of each item would be meticulously noted on a scrap piece of paper and then added to give the total for payment.

When it came to butcher shops things were very different! The garage size shop was, when compared to other shops, very empty. It was simply furnished with a large wooden topped chopping and cutting bench. A rack on one wall held the various butchery instruments and a number of large hooks hung down from the ceiling which were used to hang the animal carcases on. Sometimes a carcase was enclosed in a muslin cover but, cover or no cover, they were always covered from top to bottom with huge black flies! The butcher in our area of town only sold lamb, goat and beef and, unlike in the UK, the meat was only cut from the carcase when it was bought. The meat was butchered as you watched and waited. One thing we quickly learnt was that everything was priced the same whatever portion of the animal was purchased. Prime steak cost the same as any other portion of the animal. After we got over the dual "problems" of hygiene and flies we really enjoyed our steaks. I mention hygiene as on several occasions when we went to our local butchers we found him outside mending his car. Then when called to serve he simply wiped his oil covered hands on an equally oily rag and got straight to work on the meat.

This butcher lived just round the corner from our flat and we got to know him quite well as not only did we purchase his wares but passed his shop several times a day in our comings and goings and there would always be mutual greetings as we passed by. He introduced us to his oldest son who was soon to go to the USA to study and we met up with him several times so he could practice his English. When the time came for his son to leave Jordan for college in the USA we were invited to his farewell gathering. So late one afternoon saw Doreen and myself at his home. Doreen was quickly ushered into a room where all the ladies were sitting and I was directed into the room where the men were all gathered. They were all seated on chairs around the periphery of the room and following the custom I circled the room greeting and shaking the hand of each man in turn as the butcher proudly introduced each person to me and at the same time he told me what their employment was – it turned out that nearly everyone present worked for the secret police with some being the "head" in such and such a town or an area of Jordan.

I had already found out that his daughter worked for the secret police and had already benefited from this fact but little did I know that nearly all his extended family were part of that much feared establishment. Was our friendly butcher himself also a secret policemen who was an "undercover" operative?

I will never know!

7

A Dream and a Visit

Our new flat was one of only two found on the fourth and top floor of a building owned by the Assyrian Orthodox Church. Located near the top of one of the seven hills that Amman was built on, it commanded an uninterrupted panoramic view over the city.

We settled into the flat several days before Christmas and our new neighbours, who we were told were a local Palestinian family, moved into their new home several days after Christmas. Our first introduction to them was when, without warning, our front door opened and in came a man, a woman and two very young children. The oldest child was holding onto the woman's skirt whilst she carried a baby in her arms. The woman plonked herself down on a chair and proceeded to breast feed her baby while at the same time they introduced themselves as our new neighbours. Jojo and Labeeb were to be good neighbours and become good friends. The two doors were adjacent to each other and when we were in they were never locked. The doors opened straight into the lounge. Our neighbours came in and out at will and we were expected to do the same with them. They kept a good friendly eye on us and always made themselves aware and were "interested" in who visited us. We had a steady stream of visitors as part of our language learning process was to visit people and in turn be visited by them to help build up our language and cultural sensitivity skills.

After we had been living there for a few months it just so happened that one night Doreen had a dream and woke up concerned and disturbed as she remembered it. She dreamt that one day our flat door opened and in came a man who we did not know. He was dressed completely in black. What was particularly noticeable was that he had a very dark menacing manner about him. Unlike most dreams Doreen could not get it out of her mind and it troubled her. As the day progressed she voiced the fact that we should be careful about who we invited or encouraged to visit us.

Late that same afternoon, at the time one could expect any visitors to come, the door opened and two young men walked straight into our lounge. They were not known to us and, as such, should not have just come right in uninvited – they should have knocked on the door and waited to be invited in.

Local culture and custom, although already flouted by them, dictated that we welcome them. So we exchanged names and small talk and because they were men Doreen absented herself as much as possible and after the first introductions just brought refreshments to us as hospitality demanded. They said that they had heard that we lived here and wanted to welcome us. They freely told us they worked for the secret police and could supply us with a whole range of food at cut prices and proceeded to give us a very large box of groceries and some toys for the boys. A small token gift would have been perfectly acceptable but this was something else and warning bells began to ring in our heads. Doreen quietly whispered to me what I was thinking – we must not accept their gift. So we thanked them for their kind gift but said it was far too generous of them but, after a while, we accepted some biscuits and small inexpensive toys for each of our boys. Face had been saved!

The visit progressed and I was then horrified when one of them produced his hand gun and proceeded to show it to our seven year old son. It was not done in any menacing way but it just was not right or acceptable as far as we were concerned. Earlier when Doreen brought in the fruit juice, that we always first served to visitors shortly after they arrived, one said to her in a very low voice "we know who you are and all about you - you're not English" – again a strange thing to say. After a while it was time to indicate to them that the visit should end. The acceptable and usual way to do this was to serve coffee. That done they prepared to depart. We thanked them for their visit and said they were welcome to come again but if they did they should bring their mother or sister with them so that

Doreen could stay in the room and be fully part of the visit.

So they left and could not have been down much more than one flight of stairs before our neighbour, Labeeb, was through our door like a flash wanting to know why the two young men had visited us. "They are very bad men" he said and it was good we did not accept all their gifts. He insisted that if they came again we were to come and get him to be with us.

We never saw them again.

Was Doreen's dream a supernatural God directed incident or just a coincidental occurrence?

8

Jordanian Friends and Neighbours

We had only been living in our flat in the Assyrian Orthodox Church compound a few weeks when, on answering a knock on the door, we opened it to find the local priest, who lived in a flat in an adjoining block, had once again come to visit us. This time though, next to him stood another fully robed Assyrian priest who he introduced us to as his cousin. It turned out that he was also the Assyrian Orthodox Archbishop of Jerusalem. The St. Marks Assyrian Church and monastery in Jerusalem where he lived is recognised by many as housing the location of the "upper room". The "room" was in the house of Mary the mother of Mark, the writer of the gospel bearing his name. It was here Jesus celebrated the Last Supper with His disciples and where the disciples were gathered together again when the Holy Spirit came upon them, on the Day of Pentecost, as promised by Jesus before He ascended into heaven.

At that time the land border between the Israeli occupied West Bank and the Kingdom of Jordan was firmly closed except for very high ranking religious personnel. The Archbishop was one such person and made regular trips to visit all the churches under his jurisdiction in the Middle East. He became a regular visitor to our home because whenever he passed through Amman he would drop in to see us. He was particularly delighted to learn that our oldest son was called Mark and was very insistent that we be his all-expenses paid guests in St Mark's monastery in Jerusalem one Easter time. Although we would have loved to have done so unfortunately, for various reasons, we were not able to take him up on his offer.

After we got to know our immediate neighbours we learned that there had been a major "fallout" in their wider family and that a reconciliation gathering and meal was planned. We were instructed that we had to attend the get together with them. We were not sure if this was to act as independent observers and go-betweens or were we to be present, hopefully to prevent any further escalation of the conflict! All seemed to depart happy and we got to meet the extended family of our neighbours and they in turn got to meet us. Only a little later the wider family again brought us into their affairs once more. They asked us to vet a young couple from America who wanted to offer a new home to a young distant relative then living in a Christian run orphanage in the West Bank. We felt honoured to be included in their deliberations as to the future of the young orphan girl but were aware that we were not in a position to give definitive advice and could only offer suggestions as to how they should proceed and to pray with them that the right decision would be made.

Then another neighbour asked Doreen to pray for her that her unborn child would be a boy. In a culture where giving birth to a boy was greatly celebrated whereas giving birth to a girl was often viewed unhappily, this mother to be, who already had two girls was desperate for a son. This desperation stemmed from the fact that her husband said, and he was serious, that he would divorce her and send her back to her family if the desired for boy did not arrive this time round. There was great rejoicing when a baby boy was born.

The city of Amman, like Rome, is said to be built on seven hills so one was forever going up and down hill. On the way back from shopping one day Doreen was struggling to manoeuvre a pushchair with a baby in it whilst at the same time carry heavy grocery shopping bags. Then, it just so happened that, a local woman drew alongside her and taking one of the large shopping bags said that she would give her a helping hand. She said that she could see that Doreen had a cross round her neck and that she liked her because of that.

On reaching our apartment block they then struggled up the ninety one stairs to our flat. Naturally she was asked in for some refreshment and together they chatted for a while. So began an acquaintance with her, her husband and several small children who all resided in one small cramped room. It turned out that her husband was the itinerant local cobbler who hauled his workshop cart around the streets all day long touting for business. They were part of the nominal Christian community but had not attended a place of worship for a very long time. We encouraged them to come to the church we attended, that was in fact very near their home, and were delighted when they did so.

Our immediate neighbours were also members of the Christian community but, like the shoe and sandal mender had not attended any church in years. As our friendship developed first Jojo and the two daughters started to come to church with us and then the Sunday came when Labeeb announced that he would come with us.

So off we went together and as we climbed the outside steps to get to the road rats were scurrying everywhere. One emboldened fat rat came too close and Labeeb whipped off his sandal and hit it firmly on the head. With a screech it turned and ran away and we continued on our way to church.

Now at that time in Jordan in a church service the women and children would sit on one side of the church and the men would sit together on the other side. So it turned out that I sat right next to Labeeb. A short time into the service Labeeb started to shake with seemingly uncontrollable laughter. It was obvious that he was having trouble staying quiet. I nudged him while at the same time whispering "Shush, what's the matter with you?" To which he replied, "I was thinking of that rat – I bet it has a bad headache!"

Long after we left Amman we heard that Jojo and the girls had become regular members of the church and also Labeeb would be seen there from time to time.

9

A Surprise Proposal

At any time of the day we could expect our next door neighbours, particularly Jojo the woman, to come into to our flat. It might be for a chat, it might be so her children could play with ours but often it was just out of curiosity to see what Doreen was doing. She was intrigued to see Doreen studying the reading and writing of Arabic. In some ways these visits were quite burdensome as they took up a lot of our time that sometimes we felt could be used in a better way. However soon Doreen had an idea. As part of our language study we were reading through the gospel of John so Doreen asked Jojo to help her with the pronunciation of the Arabic. It turned out that Jojo had obviously had very little education and found reading difficult. So together they sat helping each other – Doreen helping Jojo to read the words of the gospel and Jojo helping Doreen with the correct pronunciation of those life giving words.

Jojo and Labeeb had two daughters but it became obvious to us that the youngest was the father's favourite. Then after we had lived in the flat for a little over a year, late one afternoon, Labeeb came through the door, not dressed in his work clothes as was usually the case but, dressed in his best clothes. We had reached the point in our speaking of Arabic that, because our Arabic was better than his very limited use of English, our conversations now took place in Arabic. Nevertheless I still had to concentrate really, really hard in order to understand what people were saying and often did not immediately grasp what was being said. As we talked that afternoon I suddenly understood why Labeeb had come to talk dressed in his best attire. It just so happened that he was proposing that we make a marriage contract between our two families! His proposal was that our oldest son, Mark, marry his favourite youngest daughter – now two years old and six years younger that our son. However there were to be some caveats to the contract that had to be fulfilled before they married. On our side Mark must be qualified as a doctor or an engineer and Labeeb on his side would provide a fully furnished home and a Mercedes car that he would bring from Germany. At first I thought that he was joking with me as he often did but realised with growing horror and concern that this was not the case – he was being completely serious.

Help Lord - how do I reply to this and still remain good friends with our lovely neighbours? I must admit that I cannot remember exactly what I said but it went along the lines that I was honoured that he had suggested this alliance. I mentioned the big gap in their ages. I said that in England we allowed our children to choose their career so I could not guarantee the doctor or engineer request. I mentioned that shortly we were due to leave Amman and that Mark would most likely be working in England when he grew up and was qualified in his chosen profession. I ended by saying that I felt that the two children were too young for us to make any binding agreement and perhaps we should delay considering this for the moment. Thankfully Labeeb got the message and was quite happy with the outcome as I had not made an outright refusal of the proposal – face had been saved. The matter was never mentioned again in the remaining months we spent in Amman.

How I pitched the reply, just right as it turned out, I will never know.

Was it a supernatural God inspired reply or just a coincident that the right words were used?

10

Medical Matters

One of the consequences of living abroad, and indeed at that time of any overseas travel, involved the matter of inoculations for protection from diseases and illnesses not likely to be contracted in the UK. These were not one off vaccinations but had to be repeated every few years. This was the one thing I dreaded as I had a real aversion to needles. This was probably due to the fact that as a six to eight year old child I had had to endure many courses of injections. Back then the needles were not like the disposable thin ones that are used now but big thick reusable ones. Then even though the doctor assured me that she had especially sharpened the needle for me it made no difference to the way I viewed them – even as an adult! My boys were rather amused at their father's dislike of injections and always made sure I was the first in the family line up to receive a vaccination when needed – just in case I fainted and required time to recover!

One day a wrong movement when relocating a very heavy piece of office equipment caused my back to "go". I lay on the office floor in agony for over an hour before I was able to get up and into a car to be driven home. Back home the only "comfortable" place for me was the floor and even then any slight movement was accompanied with excruciating pain. After some time, ignoring my protestations, Doreen called our doctor. On seeing the state I was in out came his syringe to give me some pain relief. As I turned my face away, so I could not see the approaching needle, I glimpsed the three grinning faces of my boys peering through a gap in the doorway wanting to see their dad's reaction.

During all the years abroad the family suffered the usual illnesses of family life but some incidents do stick in our minds for various reasons. Visits to Egypt always held the distinct possibility of an upset digestive system and diarrhoea and on one such occasion this was accompanied by extreme aching of the whole body. After making it back to our home in Cyprus over the next few hours the pain progressively got worse. The assistant director of MECO was a doctor with a wealth of experience of working in the area and fairly quickly determined that I had contracted dengue fever that is spread by mosquito bites. Another name for the condition is break-bone fever due to the pain felt in the limbs and joints. After a long period in bed getting over the condition when I eventually was able to get up I was hardly able to even walk and it took several weeks to gain strength. But, gain strength I did.

In Jordan on another occasion I succumbed to what I think was a very bad case of flu. For several days I was confined to bed and found that I slept most of the time.

One afternoon I woke up and was startled, and at first alarmed, to find several men attired in dark suits looking just like undertakers standing round my bed. Gratefully they were from a local church that had heard that I was unwell and had come to visit and pray for me. However our neighbour assured Doreen that she had a cure for my ailing body. So Doreen followed her into her kitchen to see her concoct the "medicine". An assortment of leaves were taken out of a collection of jars and placed in a small saucepan of water and boiled. The thoroughly boiled and strained water was then decanted into a mug, allowed to cool and brought through to me to drink. The two ladies then stood over me to ensure that I drank down every last drop. The taste was horrific beyond words but my condition did improve. I jokingly put this down to the fact that I was threatened with a second terrible dose if I did not get better quickly. The real truth though I believe was the fact that many people both expatriate and local Christians were praying for my state of health.

Although we and others frequently prayed that we would keep in good health on occasions our only recourse, in fact, was to pray. In Jordan late one night, it just so happened that, our eighteen month old son woke up and started to cry. It was not his normal waking up cry but one laced with pain. The intense crying was not alleviated in any way when he was picked up and we became alarmed when it appeared that the whole of his left side was paralysed. Then he was sick and also his temperature was very high indeed. What should we, what could we do? We were without transport in a strange city with no idea where good doctors could be found at that time of night. As for hospitals – a doctor friend at language school had recently advised that he did not recommend anyone use the hospital in our area as conditions in it were extremely bad due to a current cholera epidemic. Nearby lived a fellow language school student who was also a doctor. Having roused him from his bed he hurried over to our flat. A thorough examination did not reveal or even suggest a possible cause of our son's distressing condition and there was no more that he could do or suggest medically. At that time of night the only other course of action was for us to pray – so standing round his bed we asked the Lord to bring peace and healing to our suffering child. In the morning although it seemed that the pain had abated he still could not use the left side of his body. Later that morning after seeing a succession of doctors we were none the wiser as to what was still ailing our son. Perhaps a dislocated shoulder or hair line fracture was one suggestion but x rays were negative. Over the next week he very slowly regained the use of his arm and leg and was able to once again walk properly. Only years later did the likely cause of this episode come to light. Back in England on two separate occasions, due to our son's hearing loss, we were thoroughly quizzed regarding his medical history. On describing his condition that night and his road to recovery in the days that followed both doctors pronounced that he almost certainly had had encephalitis. "I think you should be grateful your son survived with his life and without severe brain damage" commented one of the doctors.

As well as our own prayers in the midst of medical emergencies we often requested in our letters to those around the world whose prayers supported us in our work that they specifically pray for our safety and good health. Were the incidents described above ones where these prayers were answered?

Then again our bodies are "fearfully and wonderfully made" by God and have the inbuilt natural ability to heal themselves even if sometimes it takes time and medication. But we also believe that sometimes God heals miraculously.

On several occasions in our lives the line between the body healing "naturally" and God supernaturally intervening in the situation to bring healing and restoration has been crossed. What side of the line would you place each of the situations described above?

11

Jordanian Driving Licence

Although I knew, before we left England, that we would not have a car in Jordan, one day when exploring Amman on foot I came to the offices of the Royal Automobile Club of Jordan and decided to obtain an International Driving Licence just in case it was ever needed.

Having got it I then found out that if one had Jordanian residency one was not allowed to use an International Driving Licence locally. This meant that I had to get a Jordanian driving licence in order to be able to drive a car in the country. So, when after we had lived in Jordan for a few months MECO decided to send a car from Lebanon for the MECO workers in Amman to use, it was imperative that I procure a Jordanian Driving Licence.

Obtaining any official document was always looked upon with dread as there seemed to be so many "hoops to jump through" in order to achieve the objective of getting that small coveted laminated card. Nobody I asked was able, for sure, to tell me the procedure for obtaining a licence. Suggestions varied. Some said I would have to take a road test. Some said I could just exchange my British Licence or my International Licence for a Jordanian one. Some said I would simply have to pay a bribe to an official in the issuing office! As for any forms in Arabic to fill in nobody had an answer.

So it was, that with some trepidation, early one morning I went to the office where I was told licences were issued. Outside there was a melee of people waiting to get inside the building. Now, at some government offices, there were men who would offer, for a fee of course, to guide and help you through the process of obtaining whatever you were at that office to get. So after a bit of haggling a price was agreed with a man who was able to communicate in English. He produced forms in Arabic and proceeded to fill them in in Arabic for me – something I would not have been able to do. He told me that he would persuade the official to waive the need for a road test as I had both a UK and an International Licence to show them. He then led me through the crowd into the offices and attracted the attention of an official at one of the decks who he greeted, as was the custom, with a hearty handshake and kisses on both cheeks and many, many words of greeting. Greetings completed, they then had a short animated conversation after which my helper turned to me and said "No road test today – just a medical."

So off to the "doctor" I was led. The medical turned out to simply be an eye test. Fortunately I did not have to read Arabic letters off the sight test board on the wall because it had no letters on it. The test board was set out in the same way as in England but instead of different letters of the alphabet it simply has rows of "C"s – each row a different size. But the "C"s had openings to the left and right and to the top and bottom. The eye test comprised of reading along the line and saying which way the opening of the "C" was orientated. I was thankful that by this time I knew the Arabic words for Left, Right, Top and Bottom. I passed with flying colours!

Next came the official photograph and then the licence card was ready to have the personal details filled in by hand. The card was almost completed, all in Arabic script, when the official said "All I need now is your blood group in case of accident". It was a question I did not have the answer to and the requirement was quite unexpected. When I said that I did not know my blood group the official waved his hand in the air, said "no matter" and wrote something on the licence card.

Then off the card went to be laminated and so, after a four hour marathon through officialdom, I was soon on my way home with my Jordanian Driving Licence.

On inspecting the licence I saw that the official had written that I was blood group B+. This was a little worrying if this information was ever to be used but my fears were somewhat allayed when a couple of doctor friends at language school both informed me that no self-respecting doctor would ever use it as a basis for a blood transfusion without first checking its authenticity.

I just thank the Lord that no accident caused my doctor friends statement to be tested and now over forty years later I still do not know my blood group!

12

Car Importation Permit

After we had lived in Amman for a number of months new people joined us and as the number of our colleagues had doubled MECO decided that we should be provided with a car for communal use. At that time there was an old VW Beetle car in Lebanon that was not being used so it was decided that someone would bring it from Beirut, through Syria, to us in Jordan.

At the Syrian / Jordanian boarder the car was allowed in as a temporary import and the relevant document was provided. The importation document lasted for six months and we were told that sometimes a one month extension to the initial document could be obtained but that was at the whim of the official dealing with the matter at the time. After that a heavy import tax would have to be paid if the car remained in Jordan even for a day longer.

As the six months drew to an end application was made to renew the importation document and the official grudgingly gave a one month extension when we pointed out to him that this had been done for friends of ours in the past so why not for us now.

So for some seven months both ourselves and our colleagues enjoyed being able to drive out of the built up capital of Amman and visit some of the historic and Biblical sites to be found in Jordan. We were renewed, refreshed and revived by the fresh air and beauty of the Jordanian countryside, forests and desert places.

As the seven months of car use was coming to the end we were unhappy at the prospect of losing this life enriching mode of transport. But although we did not know of anyone who had managed to keep a car importation document for more than the initial six months and then an extra month's extension we still decided to apply for a further extension.

With much prayer I returned to the government office with the documentation. As soon as the official saw the paperwork he said that no more extensions were possible and that we would have to take the car permanently out of the country or pay the large importation tax. I tried to persuade him to let us extend for just another month but he said he would get into trouble with his superior if he were to do that. Then, it just so happened that, hardly without thinking, on the spur of the moment, I asked if I could talk to his superior who turned out to be the Under-Secretary for Customs. The official smiled, laughed and said "He is a very hard man and will never let you keep the car here any longer. But I will ask if he will meet you".

With that he sent a "runner" off to his boss with my request to speak with him.

Back came the "runner" who escorted me upstairs to another much more luxurious office. This new official spoke perfect English and I explained our predicament, that the car was used to explore the wonderful Jordanian countryside and simply said I would be very grateful if he would allow us to extend the importation of the car a little longer. To my surprise he simply said, "No problem this time but after this no more." With that he scribbled something in Arabic on a piece of paper that I could not read and said "Take this back downstairs and the man will extend your document".

So down I went and gave the paper to the official who looked at it once, then twice and then, in Arabic, exclaimed to a colleague "What's this? I don't believe it. He's given not one month but a two month extension – I've never known this before." "Oh, sometimes he changes the rules for religious people" replied his colleague.

Was that a supernatural God incident and an answer to our need and our prayers?

I know what I think, but you be the judge.

13

Journey Planning With a Welcome Surprise

The VW Beetle car we had used in Jordan for some nine months took us or our colleagues out of the busy, noisy, often dusty and claustrophobic capital city of Amman. We really appreciated being able to use it. However the old car frequently caused concern as it broke down quite often. It was never ever anything really big or expensive but we were fearful that one day it would need a major repair with an accompanying major expense. The car was so old and worthless that any big repair bill would be difficult to justify. However because it was in the country as a temporary import there would be major problems if there was a major breakdown as it would either have to be removed from the country or import duty, as if it were a new car, would have to be paid. Duty would have to be paid even if the car was a write-off or had even been scrapped. So in some ways we were glad when it finally had to be returned to its home in Lebanon.

The civil war in Lebanon at that time was such that it was not deemed safe for me to drive it into and then through Beirut and up into the mountains to the home of our leader in Lebanon. This was because I had no idea where his home was or how to find it in the mountain town where he lived. (Remember there was no "sat nav" or even good road maps of Lebanon forty years ago). Also, even if directions were obtained, any possible safe directed route could change at a moment's notice. So it was decided that I would drop it off at a Christian hospital way up in the mountains fairly near to the main Damascus to Beirut highway many miles from Beirut itself. Then colleagues would be informed of its arrival and would collect it from the hospital. I, and the person who was to accompany me on the drive, would then travel by shared taxi back to Amman. It was not an ideal situation but the only sensible one.

Our departure date was decided and in the afternoon the day before our journey it just so happened that there was a knock on our door. It was a man, who we did not know, who was working with a Christian group in Lebanon. He said that he had heard that I was driving to Beirut the next day and if that was true could we go in a convoy of two cars as he did not really want to travel alone. He had driven his car to Jordan to find accommodation in Amman as he was pulling out of Lebanon due to the worsening situation in the country but wanted to go back to collect the rest of his belongings and then return to Jordan.

As we spoke further we really sensed that God's hand was in this. He lived in the mountain town where ideally we had wanted to take the car and he knew exactly where our Lebanon team leader lived. He also knew very well various alternative routes that we could take if the need arose because of fighting or temporary blocked roads. Also we could return to Jordan with him instead of getting a shared taxi. Then, almost as a bonus, when we told him that we needed to visit the Australian Embassy in Damascus on the way to Beirut he informed us that he could lead us to the area of Damascus where the embassy was situated as it was near to a hotel that he often stayed in.

We arranged to leave together early the next morning.

A supernatural God incident or a coincident?

14

Registration of a Birth

I and a colleague were prepared for a day long drive from Amman in Jordan to a mountain town, situated high up above Beirut, in Lebanon. On the way a stop off to do some business in Damascus in Syria was scheduled. Only the afternoon before, to our surprise and delight, we had arranged to travel together with a man who was returning to Lebanon in his own car and knew the way well as opposed to ourselves who had no experience of the route we should take.

We set off at the crack of dawn and together quickly travelled north towards the Syrian border. We were grateful that border formalities were completed relatively quickly and we were on the road to Damascus. When we reached the outskirts of Damascus the person who was following us in his car took over the lead and led us into the district where most of the foreign embassies were located. While our travelling companion in the other car rested in the coffee shop of an international hotel I and my colleague located the nearby Australian Embassy. My Australian colleague had recently been blessed with the birth of a baby girl and we were now going to register her birth and so obtain the coveted and needed

Australian birth certificate. We had to do this in Damascus as Australia did not have an embassy in Jordan.

We grew concerned when the staff at the embassy informed us that the person who registered births was not present and was in fact out of the country on holiday. However they said that they would do the registration if they could find the Registration Book and the blank birth certificates. So into the relevant office we went. Cupboards, drawers and even a safe were opened but to no avail as the book and documents were nowhere to be found. The embassy staff were very apologetic but said that there was nothing further they could do. We suggested that we could drop by again on the way back to Jordan in a couple of days-time but were told that the person responsible would still be on holiday and they did not know how to contact him. As, rather dejectedly, we prepared to leave one of the embassy staffed rushed up to the person we were dealing with and said that it just so happened that the "Registrar" was, unexpectedly, on the telephone. We never knew the reason why he saw the need to contact his embassy while on his holiday but were overjoyed that he was able to tell the staff where the necessary paperwork to complete our visit was to be found. Soon we were on our way to Lebanon again – the new birth certificate carefully packed.

Having collected our friend from the hotel we made good time along the main highway to the Lebanese border. Once in Lebanon our friend became the lead car again and after we had traversed the Bekaa valley and then began to climb up into the mountains he quickly branched off the main road and we continued on our way along a series of narrow precipitous mountainous roads that eventually brought us to our destination without having to go anywhere near Beirut and into the more potentially dangerous and problematic areas of the country. Our Lebanese leader got the surprise of his life when we turned up on his doorstep but was very grateful that he would not have to go and collect the car from miles away over the mountains.

A supernatural God incident or was the perfect, unexpected, timing of a telephone call just a coincident?

15

A Family Visit to Lebanon

When we answered the Lord's call to work in the Middle East it soon became clear that the most likely place of work would be in the country of Lebanon where MECO was associated with five Christian schools. The only possible problem about this location was that there was an ongoing civil war in the country. However if Lebanon proved an impossible destination there were other countries in the Middle East where we could be of use – Egypt being the most likely alternative. By the time it came for us to leave England intermittent bouts of fighting had been taking place in Lebanon for two years but it was hoped that, during the two years we would be in Jordan for language and cultural studies, there would be an end to the civil war so paving the way for us to indeed work in Lebanon.

Now, after a year and a half of living in Jordan there was still no let-up in the civil war in Lebanon and a decision had to be made as to whether this was to be our place of work. The schools there were still open for most of the time and there was definitely a "place" for us there. So it was decided that the whole family should visit the country for a few days to get a feel as to what it would be like to live there particularly in such a volatile situation.

Early one morning we left Amman in a shared, long wheel base, Mercedes taxi. The driver, our family of five and three strangers settled down for the one hundred and twenty five mile drive to Damascus. Although the driving time was around three hours border formalities added another hour to the journey. In Damascus we had to change to another shared taxi. Like all the other Damascus to Beirut taxis on the stand, unlike the plush car that had brought us from Jordan, it was a rather battered vehicle sporting a couple of bullet holes in the windscreen! So, with some trepidation, we motored for two and a half hours the eighty five miles into Beirut. The taxi dropped us off, opposite the residence of the British Ambassador, at the School for the Blind where we were warmly welcomed by the leader of our workers in Lebanon. Then we were off again up into the mountains above Beirut to stay at his family home.

As our children played with our hosts children in the cool safety of the mountain town where he lived Doreen and myself were introduced to the mechanics of working in the schools and living in the country. We were shocked by the many roadblocks and checkpoints manned by motley collections of armed men and women. We were saddened to see buildings shattered by tank and field gun fire. We noticed that the majority of buildings in certain areas were riddled with bullet holes. But amid this life was going on in an uneasy normal way. On a couple of occasions we were treated to a symphony of heavy gunfire and one night we were wakened by the booms as big guns opened up in the distance. Our hosts admitted that, before our visit, they did not know whether their prayers should be that there was no fighting or gunfire to be heard or if it were better that we were "treated" to the sounds of civil war that they had been hearing for the past four years.

As our time in the country came to an end we became convinced that this was the place where we were destined by the Lord to live when our language study in Jordan had come to an end. We now had to return to Jordan to plan our move to Lebanon.

16

An Unwelcome Situation

Just as we had come to Lebanon by shared service taxi so was our return journey to be the same way. At the school where I was going to teach in Lebanon we bade farewell to our host who handed us over to a colleague to take us to catch a service taxi. From the Christian area of Beirut he drove us into the Muslim area and stopped just outside the rubble of no-man's land. He pointed down a side road to where a couple of large cars were parked and said "This is where service taxis used to go from". Then pointing to the cars parked down the road said "I think those are taxies. Go down and see".

As I approached the cars I looked back to see that Doreen, our three young boys and our luggage was now out on the pavement beside his car. On enquiry the cars turned out to be private cars and not taxies. However the men standing by them told me where the service taxies now ran from and how to get there.

As I turned to return to our car a volley of gunfire broke out quite nearby and a few seconds later, to my horror, I saw my colleague jump into his car and drive off at speed up the road leaving our family standing on the pavement as gunfire continued nearby.

Behind me a man shouted "come quickly" and opened the door of his car for me to get in. Back up the road we drove, bundled Doreen, the boys and luggage into his car and he then drove us to the service taxi stand some distance away.

Our colleague's irresponsible reaction to the gunfire showed us how living in an uncertain situation can cloud and influence ones judgement and make one act in a dangerous and irrational way – he just should never have left us stranded in what for us all was a hazardous and unknown situation in a city we did not know at all.

But it also showed us the kindness and help that could come from complete strangers who were concerned to keep others safe in times of trouble. It also, I believed, showed us that we could cope in similar stressful situations if they were to arise in the future and furthermore that the Lord could be trusted to keep us safe and provide a way out for us in times of trouble.

Soon we were driving out of Beirut up the main highway into and over the mountains towards Damascus. The windows of the taxi were firmly closed because not only was it quite cold the higher we climbed but it also began to drizzle with rain.

Apart from music blaring from a radio we were, every few minutes, subjected to the sound of the taxi driver clearing his throat, winding his window down, spitting out of it and then winding it up again accompanied by the exclamation "Oh Lord"! We were glad when we reached Damascus and changed taxis. The rest of the journey, back home to Amman in Jordan, through Syria was uneventful.

17

Moving Home – Jordan to Lebanon

At first sight it looked as if our house move from Jordan to Lebanon would prove logistically much more difficult than our move from England to Jordan. Shipping our baggage by sea was obviously a non-starter as the Beirut port was for all intents and purposes closed to civilian freight. As well as the cost, taking all our belongings as excess baggage by air was an impossibility. We also knew that the cost of air freight was notoriously very expensive.

Therefore we decided that this relocation would entail moving both ourselves and our goods overland to Lebanon at the same time. We concluded that the best way to do this was to hire two service taxies exclusively for our use and pile ourselves and all our goods into and onto each taxi. We did not relish the thought of customs checks when we left Jordan and another shortly after on entry to Syria. Then offloading the taxies in Damascus and onto another two taxies bound for Lebanon. This would be followed again with customs checks as we left Syria and again as we entered Lebanon. But that plan seemed to be the best option and friends and colleagues agreed with us. We now just needed to decide on a date for our move taking into account the fact that about the same time the family was required to attend a conference in Cyprus.

While we were still looking into the logistics of our move a friend asked me to go with him to the airport in Amman to help get some goods that had been sent to him from the USA. I do not remember how but it just so happened that I got talking to one of the people in the Jordanian Alia Airline department and mentioned that I was moving to Lebanon but was going by road. When asked why I was not flying I said that it would be just too expensive as the family had so much luggage to go with them. "But if you fly to Beirut yourself and send all your belongings as unaccompanied excess baggage the cost of the excess will be very, very small" said the clerk. "But I have many, many kilos" I replied, "how much will each kilo cost?" When his reply came I did not believe I was hearing correctly and asked him to repeat the cost. He did so and went on to comment that their aircraft, at that time, were flying from Amman to Beirut with their cargo holds virtually empty and with hardly any passengers as "nobody wants to go to Beirut at the moment – we only go as we always have a completely full plane coming back". Hence the cost of a non-return passenger ticket had been dramatically reduced and freight or excess baggage was carried at the incredibly low cost of literally a few pence per kilo.

It also turned out that due to an anomaly in the pricing of air tickets we would be able to fly to Lebanon with a "side trip flight" to Cyprus for the same price as a simple single ticket to Beirut. In essence our flight to the Cyprus conference was "free". So it turned out that moving by air with all our household chattels would cost us far less than if we had stuck with our original plan to go by road. Furthermore it would be a whole lot less stressful as well!

Our home in Amman packed up and numerous goodbyes said we headed for the airport very, very early one morning. All our goods were packed in an array of suitcases, travel trunks and big boxes ready for their journey. The first plane of the day to Beirut departed with all our luggage and I followed it on another plane a little later that day after I had first seen Doreen and the boys off to Cyprus on yet another aircraft. I would then join them in a couple of days after our goods had arrived safely in Beirut and I had had time to get them cleared from customs.

Having flown to Beirut I was met at the airport by the colleague who had abandoned us on our last trip to the capital. He then redeemed himself in a big way as he guided me through the process of getting all our baggage cleared through customs in the freight hangers at Beirut airport. With that process completed he haggled the price down for the hire of a small pickup truck and its driver to take our goods to our new home high up in the hills overlooking the city of Beirut.

Job done, the next day I flew off to join the rest of the family for the conference in Cyprus. Together we would come back to begin the next chapter of our lives in Lebanon.

18

Crossing Points

Between 1975 and 1990, during the civil war in Lebanon, when driving anywhere and at any time, it was usual to encounter road blocks and checkpoints. Sometime the road blocks were simply acting as checkpoints so that your papers and vehicle could be examined but at other times they were there, as their name implied, to block any traffic from entering a particular area. At checkpoints the road was not blocked at all but you had to slow down enough for the people manning it to see who you were and wave you on or wave you to the side to be "searched". Some checkpoints had a chicane, made of big old oil barrels filled with concrete or just big concrete blocks while others simply consisted of high banks of sand, earth and building rubble that you had to slowly make your way through. As you drove along you came under the scrutiny of the armed men or women manning them.

Beirut itself was divided into a predominantly Christian East part and a predominantly Muslim West part and was under the control of some eighteen different militias. The Lebanese army and the Syrian army were also present at some of the most strategic places. Each group administered and controlled its own enclave. The line of division between East and West was known as the green line – probably named because of the "river of green colour" caused by the profusion of long grass, shrubs and even small trees that had sprang up in the deserted area of the line that divided Beirut. Nearly all the roads crossing the green line were firmly blocked off with permanent metal barriers, large concrete blocks or towering banks of sand along with the rubble of war torn buildings. There were only ever five crossing points between East and West separated by an area of no man's land. At any one time the number of crossings open could vary from all of them to none of them! The area of the crossings were filled with comprehensively war damaged buildings and were heavily fortified. They were frequently closed to traffic of any sort because snipers were often at work somewhere or another along the line. Sniper fire or the unstable political state of the day accounted for the frequent opening and closing of the crossings. When crossing, one never lingered in the no man's land and would only cross if there was a steady flow of traffic crossing as well as yourself. At the crossing checkpoint itself cars would only ever proceed at walking pace until waved on their way.

At one of the crossing points however there was an exception to that rule. This particular crossing took you over an elevated section of road about a kilometre long and was notorious for sniper fire so was avoided if at all possible. Those manning this checkpoint for outgoing traffic did not want or expect you to slow down or stop unless there was a barrier in the road that indicated that the way was completely closed. Approaching this checkpoint, if I could see no barrier was present, I would pick up speed and drive as fast as I possibly could over the elevated road to the safety of the other side. Our boys still remember the drill of getting down into the foot-well of the car behind the front seats as we approached the crossing and only emerged when we had to slow down for the checkpoint the other side! Needless to say we only used this crossing when absolutely necessary!

Although people frequently crossed the green line for work or business there were periods of time when the situation was so volatile and unstable that a crossing was made only if it was really important to do so. There was one occasion when I found myself in that situation. There was some legal business that was being transacted in the UK that required my signature to be authenticated at the British Consulate situated in Muslim West Beirut but we lived in Christian East part of the country. A legal deadline was approaching and so I needed to travel from East Beirut to West Beirut to get to the Embassy. Early in the morning I left home knowing, from the early radio news, that all the green line crossings were either closed or "suspect". I assured Doreen that I would be careful and only cross to the other side if others were doing so. I chose to try what was known as the Sodeco crossing as not only was I very familiar with this crossing it was the one that tended to be the safest and most often open one used by me. That morning very little traffic was on the roads but as I got near the crossing checkpoint a couple of cars turned into the road in front of me and I saw that they were quickly waved through by the soldiers so I duly followed them. Safely arriving at the embassy the paperwork I had was quickly processed, signed, sealed and ready for me to send off for hand delivery to the UK curtesy of a friend travelling the next day. At that time this was the only way to get letters out of the country.

As I chatted to the consul he remarked "You normally live in Brummana don't you? Where are you staying now?" "Oh. I've come from Brummana this morning," I replied. "How?" he exclaimed, "all the crossings are closed". "But I've just used the Sodeco crossing – it wasn't very busy though", I responded. "Are you hoping to go back home today?" he then enquired. When I replied in the affirmative he asked me to hold on for a few minutes. When he returned he told me the "security people" connected to the embassy had just told him that I was lucky to have got to the Sodeco crossing at a time when it just so happened that it was open for only a few minutes. It was now firmly closed and was not expected to open anytime soon. All the other Beirut green line crossings were closed as well. After I told him the way I would attempt to return home he bade me farewell and wished me a safe, uneventful journey. And so it was that a long, long detour was made southward, then up into the mountain foothills surrounding Beirut to get around the end of the green line. It was a long but uneventful journey home.

Was the timing of crossing at Sodeco a supernatural God incident or just coincidental?

19

Air Travel Incidents

It was because of the civil war in Lebanon that the number of airlines flying to and from Beirut become very limited due to the uncertain and volatile situation in the country. On one occasion, we noted with somewhat bemusement that our aircraft travel insurance stated that "this insurance ceases immediately the aircraft wheels touch the runway at Beirut airport". When the airport was "open", such was the uncertainty of the situation that, one went to the airport and actually went through the full check in and security procedure without actually being sure that you would get on a plane that day. It was only when you boarded the bus to take you out onto the runway that you were fairly certain that your plane was in fact coming in to land.

Then the usual procedure was that as the plane was actually landing and taxiing to park up, the passengers would be transported out to join their luggage already set out in rows on the tarmac waiting for it to be individually identified before it was then immediately loaded into the aircraft hold. The incoming passengers and baggage were offloaded from the plane in double quick time and the outgoing passengers, after identifying their own luggage, were hurried onto the aircraft that then immediately took off without any delay. Such was the concern about the aircraft being targeted for shelling or hijacking.

Once when leaving Lebanon on what was identified as a direct flight to London as soon as we were airborne we were told that we were to make an unscheduled stop in Rome as there were some passengers on the plane who wanted to get off there!

After completing one of our home assignments the whole family were travelling together back to Lebanon. As was often the case our luggage was overweight but this time by only a few kilograms. As we checked in for our flight from London Gatwick airport the young lady at the check in desk took a little persuading to allow us to take our excess weight baggage without extra payment. The first leg of the flight was to Schiphol, Amsterdam airport. Then after an overnight stopover we were due to fly on to Beirut. It was when the person on the check in desk realised our final destination was Lebanon and not Amsterdam that she waived any excess baggage charges.

Stop overs in Amsterdam were always welcome as they gave us time to wind-down and relax before we got back into the hectic swing of life in Lebanon once again. The next morning in the airport we were delighted to see three other sets of Christian workers that were on their way back into the country too after holiday breaks in their various homelands. We enjoyed catching up with each other's news and sharing what we knew of the present state of Lebanon. Much had happened there, such as the invasion and occupation of a large section of the country by the Israeli army, during the few weeks that we had been out of the country. The aircraft we were to board was a large one with both economy and business class seats. It turned out that because our family had one way tickets, as opposed to most travellers who were using return tickets, we found that we had been upgraded to travel business class. We were called to board the plane first and took our luxury seats towards the front of the aircraft. Our economy class friends boarded after us and as they passed us to take their seats they told us to enjoy the superior food and service that we should get! They then moved on to take their seats in what they termed as "plebe class"!

Thank you Lord for those little extras.

20

Lockdown in Lebanon

As I sit to write, in 2020/21, here in England we are in a state of lockdown because of the Covid 19 virus pandemic. Initially there were some food shortages and all but essential travel is banned. This took me back to numerous times in Lebanon when there were often difficulties in obtaining various essential goods. Also at times travel was discouraged or completely banned by our organisation because of the volatile situation.

Then my thoughts turned to some incidents when we really sensed God's hand with us and on us for our good and our encouragement.

When we first arrived in the country we were advised to build up a supply of essential foodstuffs. So we stocked up with flour, rice and a whole variety of dried and tinned goods that would mean that we were self-sufficient for about a month. We did not have a freezer but that was no real hardship as they were almost impossible to manage as the electricity supply was intermittent and often "off" for many hours. Because of this those that had the luxury, at that time, of owning a freezer only kept enough food that could be used immediately if it was defrosted because of a long power cut.

In Lebanon there was not a food shortage as such because the shops did, in fact, have food to sell. But there were two scenarios that prevented you from shopping. Firstly, sometimes the tense and volatile situation on the ground meant that it would be very unwise to venture outside to get to the shops. Secondly, for some reason or another the militia controlling the area frequently made all shops close for days at a time.

We soon learned that two of our local grocery shops, although "closed", were "open" to selected known customers during any lockdowns demanded by the local militia – but only if you entered through the back door. The militias were very, very strict at enforcing shop closures so one had to be extra discreet and careful if going into the shop. On one such occasion Doreen needed some food items and on entering the shop found half a dozen people, who should not have been there, standing around chatting. As she entered everything went very quiet and tension gripped those present. However the tension soon dropped away when the shop-owner spoke up saying, "Don't worry. She's one of us!" and proceeded to ask her what she wanted to purchase.

It was the same shop-owner who, on another occasion, refused to let Doreen buy ice cream when she said it was for our son who had just had his tonsils removed and we wanted something soothing to entice him to eat after the operation. He explained that because of power cuts the ice cream had been melted and refrozen on many occasions and he did not want it to harm our son.

Food was never in short supply in the shops but the same could not be said of the bottled gas that we needed for both cooking and for some of our room heaters. We always tried to keep at least one full spare bottle. A time came when, for a long period of time, others could not easily source gas but we never ever lacked it – although at times we came close to running out. I said that the Lord had provided us with a "gas angel".

When first in Lebanon there was never any shortage of the commodity and I used several different gas shops to exchange my empty gas bottles for full ones. Then obtaining gas became more and more difficult and one would have to search the shops to find it. On one occasion things were particularly bad and it was completely unobtainable. We had reached the point where even our "spare"- bottle was almost empty and for several days I did the rounds of the shops but to no avail. At one I had rarely visited before I was given some hope though when the owner told me that tomorrow he would have gas for me. Next day, true to his word, there was not only one bottle but two new full bottles waiting to be collected. I quite expected that he would ask, as everyone else was doing, an inflated price for the gas but to my great surprise he only charged the normal price. As he put them in the boot of my car he told me that he would always be able to get gas for me. It just so happened that over the next weeks and months, when others were desperate for gas, he kept his word and we always had a supply and were also able to help colleagues who ran out of gas.

I know that this storekeeper was no real angel but I often wondered what, or who, motivated him to keep us supplied.

21

Lebanese Friends and Neighbours

We became friends with a retired Lebanese Armenian couple who used to be teachers. One day Doreen happened to drop by their home and heard the gentleman playing a violin. When she mentioned that one of our sons wanted to learn how to play the instrument he immediately offered to teach him. He said that it would be best to start on the mandolin and then progress to the violin. He produced a beautiful very old mandolin for him to use. Doreen accompanied our son for his lessons so she could see what was needed and so be able to help him as he practiced at home between lessons. But the old gentleman was not so gentle when it came to teaching and our son frequently had his fret playing hand hit with a ruler if a wrong note was played. Eventually it became too much for him and he stopped learning but Doreen continued to be taught until she became quite proficient on the mandolin. The teacher then decided that he would play the violin, Doreen would play the mandolin and they would go to the house of a lady who would accompany them on the piano. They drove off to another village and were ushered into a well-guarded "palace". It was then that Doreen found out that the pianist was a part of the family of one of the political leaders of the country.

One of our son's friends invited him to his birthday party and the mother, who Doreen had also become friends with at the school gate, gave instructions as to how we should find their home. She said someone would meet us in front of a restaurant in the village and that we should then follow them in our car. We duly arrived at the restaurant only to find a couple of large four by four vehicles filled with armed men waiting for us. We, in our small VW Beetle car that had definitely seen better days, were then escorted to the fortress like mansion, guarded by armed men with dogs, where our little son's friend lived. The children who were there then all went off to play somewhere by themselves whilst the adults stood around talking, drinking and eating. That afternoon we saw and heard how the boy's parents and others, also like them with great wealth, had many worries brought upon them by their wealth and an emptiness of mind, body and soul that went with it. We compared them to the poor working people that we lived amongst in Jordan who had so very little materially but seemed to live happy and fulfilled lives. We remembered how Jesus compared and talked about the rich and the poor.

"If I had known that you were missionaries I would never have made friends with you" said Karen to Doreen as they were driving back home together. They had become friends at the gate of our children's school. Their children and ours had become good friends as well and subsequently we had visited each other's homes on several occasions. They were nominal members of the Maronite Christian community but did not seem to mind that we were obviously from the Evangelical Christian community as they knew that I taught at the Evangelical School in Beirut – a school that had a very good name among the Lebanese.

It just so happened that one day Karen inquired if perhaps Doreen knew of an organisation or orphanage that could use a couple of big suitcases full of children's clothes that she wanted to dispose of. It so happened that we indeed did. Some friends of ours were in charge of a Christian run boy's orphanage that we often visited. So one day off they both went to deliver the clothes to the orphanage. Louise, the lady in charge, was absolutely delighted to receive what turned out, at that very time, to be much needed clothes for the boys. She gave thanks to and extolled the goodness of the Lord in His timely provision of their needs. She went on to talk of other occasions when, as she put it, the Lord had miraculously provided for their necessities and for those of the orphanage. Karen listened to all that was said and made no comment but as soon she got into our car and Doreen drove away from the orphanage she turned to her and said "I know David teaches but what are you really doing here in Lebanon?" Before Doreen could answer she added, "You're missionaries aren't you? If I had known that you were missionaries I would never have made friends with you". As they drove up the hill to home, Doreen simply told her how we believed that God had "spoken" to us and also "showed" us that he wanted us to live and work for Him in Lebanon. Karen left to collect her children from school deep in thought.

Initially we wondered if the friendship would cool off but it simply continued and indeed grew stronger as the weeks went by. Karen became a regular attender of a Bible study group that Doreen held in our home. In times of difficulty in the country they could be relied upon for advice and help and the friendship continued for long after we left Lebanon. Why is it that some people are at first fearful of missionaries and do not want to befriend them? I trust we were and are like all Christians should be – simply ordinary people living our lives for Jesus.

22

Learning and Examinations

The age range of a class of children in school in England would normally be about one year. In Lebanon things could be very different and the age range in a class could be as much as three or even, in rare cases, four years. This came about as an end of year examination had to be passed in order to move on to the next year's grade. For new pupils an entrance examination was used to determine the class the pupil entered irrespective of their age. As you can imagine this could cause difficulties as the pupils in the class could be very different both mentally, physically and emotionally. The older the pupil was compared to the average age of the class the more difficult it was for them as they were seen both by their class peers and by themselves as failures. Consequently the desire to move up a class each year meant that pupils, and even more so parents, would do anything to ensure that this did indeed happen whether legitimately by "crooked" means.

Teaching methods in the Middle East at that time were very "old fashioned" compared to those in England and America. Thinking a problem through in order to grasp an idea or concept rarely entered the learning process. Learning by discovery was an alien idea. The school where I taught was housed in temporary accommodation as the original purpose built school building had been destroyed in the very early days of the civil war. Because of this there was no laboratory or equipment for my teaching of science. Consequently meaningful teaching was a real challenge. Most pupils viewed learning as being able to recite what was written in the textbooks. Understanding of what was written did not seem to matter. If I asked questions to test pupils understanding I would often be confronted by blank faces but if then told on what page of the textbook the answer was to be found some of the pupils would happily and perfectly regurgitate the whole page! As examination season approached it was normal to see pupils walking in the fields or down quite roads, textbooks in hand, quietly learning whole pages of text off by heart.

When our school examination time came round the classes were all "mixed up" to ensure that there were only two or three pupils from any one class in the same examination room. It was then made sure that these pupils were well separated so that they could not communicate in any way with each other. Desks were regularly checked to ensure that no papers were left in them or stuck under them or indeed had anything, such as science formulae, written on them. We also had to ensure that no one had a sight of any of the question papers. The actual questions were often picked at random from a bank of questions previously provided by the relevant teachers. It was then my job to duplicate all the papers and safely transport them and store them at home until the day they were needed.

Some of the more dubious senior pupils sometimes would try to pressurise the teachers, by veiled threats or offers of bribes, to tell them the actual questions that had been set. One year, it just so happened that, we had reason to believe that two of the senior pupils who were very militant and active in one of the armed groups had "forced" a couple of teachers to divulge the questions that were on their papers. So, unbeknown to all except the headmaster and myself, we obtained the question papers set for use in another school and prepared them for our own school's use. At the staff briefing before the papers were to be used that day the faces of two members of staff turned ashen when we told them that we had changed the papers. We felt that our suspicions were probably true. In the examination room we made it very, very clear that, without the knowledge of the teachers, we had changed the questions that they had set to be used. When the examination had ended we noted that the two suspect pupils headed straight for two, now slightly less ashen faced, teachers and highly animated conversations ensued. We were now sure our suspicions were confirmed!

Lebanon, before independence, came under the French mandate and continued to follow the French system of schooling that culminated in the baccalaureate examinations. These exams took place in government run centres where the atmosphere was always fraught, tempers ran high and emotions were raw. One year the national army was deployed in some government examination centres because the previous year the cheating had been so blatant with the invigilators being ignored and threatened. In one centre an invigilator had actually been shot for attempting to stop the cheating and bring order into the chaos. The story is told that in another centre then when a mathematics exam was being held and the question papers had been given out the invigilator said "You will find the answers in your desks!!" Whether the story was actually true or false I don't know but at that time it was totally believable due to the unstable nature of the country.

Having said all the above the Evangelical School where I taught worked hard to bring both thought, understanding and complete honesty into the teaching and learning process. Indeed the vast majority of the pupils were intent of being the best they could be both in character, integrity and uprightness of life. Many of the pupils went on to gain high academic achievements at university both at home and abroad. They then went on to be reliable, honourable leaders in their communities, in their workplaces and in their churches.

23

Informal School Life

When we first arrived in the Middle East I noticed that many of the men often carried small "handbags". As it was a practice totally alien to me I told Doreen that it was something that I was never ever going to do – after all it was not very manly! These "handbags" did not possess carrying handles or shoulder straps but had one small strap that was looped over the man's wrist for security purposes whilst the "handbag" was firmly gripped in the hand. They in fact were more akin to a ladies clutch or evening bag. It soon however became apparent to me why they were so popular and in next to no time I purchased one that then went everywhere with me with our passports, identity cards and money safely inside and held tightly in my hand.

My little black "handbag" was in constant use and after five years it was beginning to look a little shabby so I was delighted when on a special day one of my pupils presented me with a lovely new bag. The special day in question was Teacher's Day. It was a day I had not come across before in my previous thirteen years of teaching in England. Indeed it was not until the year 1994 that the United Nations Educational, Scientific and Cultural Organisation (UNESCO) designated a

World Teacher Day. However by that time many countries were already celebrating such a day – for example Argentina started in 1915, India in 1962 Colombia in 1950 and Thailand in 1957. In Lebanon Teacher's Day can be traced back to at least 1943. As is the case in many countries on Teacher's Day the pupils and their parents showed their thanks, honour and appreciation of their teachers in many different ways. One would return home with an abundance of cards and an assortment of chocolates, biscuits, flowers and a variety of other gifts. That day the school was filled with a party like atmosphere from start to finish.

But then on some days the atmosphere in the classrooms was much more sombre. The fact that Lebanon was in the midst of a civil war was never far from one's mind. During lessons if a burst of gunfire or a salvo of shells was heard the older pupils were usually able to tell you the type of weapon being used and how far away the "action" was. All the senior pupils were expected to be active in a local militia and so had to be forgiven if they were extra weary in class because they had been manning a checkpoint or guarding the front line of their territory all the previous night.

No pupil was permitted to come to school in their militia uniform or to openly champion any one political party. The headmaster did a superb job in keeping "politics" out of the school even when heavily pressured by various people to allow them to address the senior pupils in school time. The time came when all the older pupils, if they had not already done so, were very heavily pressured to join a militia even if they had no wish to do so. It was then that some of them asked if it was right for Christians to join a militia group to fight. When this happened we always referred them to their church leaders and pastors for advice because as foreigners we did not want and indeed feel it right to give advice about such sensitive matters. Sometimes we were hard pressed for an answer when they persisted by asking "But sir, what would you do in your own country". We were able to reply that there was no clear right or wrong answer as it just so happened that the headmaster and myself had two opposing experiences. He had been a conscientious objector and had not done military national service but I, in my teenage years at school, had done five years of military training as an army cadet.

School life was so much more than simply formal teaching in the classroom. The morning and lunch breaks afforded time to interact in a much less formal way with the pupils many of whom were keen to talk and question one on a whole range of issues. Hence some days you could see yourself faced with deep moral or religious questions amidst the threat of fighting and civil war. Then other days the mood was cheerful and had a party like atmosphere such as was present on Teacher's Day

My Teacher's Day gift of a new leather bag was presented to me by a quiet but very studious twelve year old boy. Very sadly, one afternoon, only a short time later, as he and his parents hurried to get into an underground shelter he was hit by shrapnel and died. His gift, still in my possession, holds bitter sweet memories.

24

An Unusual Day at School

The 2nd April is a date that is firmly imprinted in my memory for a number of very significant reasons. It was thirty nine years ago as I write this.

It started as just another normal day at work in a Christian school situated in East Beirut in the Lebanon. After the daily morning assembly, where the song "From the rising of the sun to the going down of the same the Lord's name is to be praised" had been sung by the senior school pupils with their usual gusto and they had listened to a short Bible talk, we had all gone off to our usual lessons until morning break came.

By this time a civil war had already been in progress in Lebanon for the past six years and we had become accustomed to periodic bursts of heavy gunfire most days that usually were nothing to really worry about - unless they were nearby of course! Then less frequently we would hear the loud explosive booms of mortar or tank shells landing with their devastating effect. The norm was that after just a few shells had been fired in quick succession if everything then went quiet then after a very short time everyone would get on with their work again as if nothing had happened.

Over the time of morning school break a few very distant booms were heard but nobody took much notice of them and we prepared to go back into lessons. Then to my great surprise the headmaster, Colin, came to me and said "David, I'm getting the kindergarten and junior school children into the bomb shelter. Would you get the seniors downstairs into the safest places possible – and please hurry". Then off he hurried upstairs. This reaction, by Colin, to today's very distant explosions was completely out of character – on previous similar occasions he had just told us to carry on as usual. I couldn't understand his change of attitude but got on with the job of moving, reluctant to move, teenagers out of their classrooms on the third and fourth floors, downstairs after Colin had first led the younger ones down.

The younger children were quickly ushered down from the fifth and sixth floors into the shelter in the basement of the building and the seniors crammed themselves into short corridors off the staircase on the first, second and third floors. Within minutes tank, mortar and field gun shells were raining down on the building and indeed on the whole surrounding area. For the next two hours every few minutes there was a barrage of explosions. After the first few barrages there was no more sound of breaking glass as every window had been blown out of the building. Each barrage shook the building but several times it was so great that we were sure that it had taken a direct hit.

Meanwhile, Doreen and Colin's wife were at another school in West Beirut completely unaffected by the shelling of East Beirut. But they could hear the constant explosions and could see the smoke rising in the distance and were not only concerned for our safety and as it was obvious that we would not be able to collect them as planned had made an arrangement for a local Christian leader to take them to his home outside Beirut. From there we could collect them to go back to our homes in the mountains. We needed to communicate with each other – a thing more easily said than done in the current situation!

Now the telephone system, at that time, in the Middle East was at its best highly unreliable and in Lebanon was completely unreliable. That day the school phone where Doreen was working was out of action so they went out to see if they could locate a working phone in a local shop. One appeared to be operational so they joined a queue of people waiting to use it. Hoping and praying that the phone in my school was working they dialled the number and heard the phone ringing. It rang and rang and just as they were about to put their phone down I answered it. After the shelling started it was the one and only time that the phone was answered although up till then it had been ringing constantly!

After the shelling had been going on for quite a while a message had come up to me on the third floor that, only if I thought it safe to do so, could I get into the school office on the fourth floor to retrieve some important paperwork that Colin did not wish to be destroyed. Now for some time the shells had been coming in groups, with a short lull between them, and during one such lull I ran up the shattered glass covered stairs to the office where the telephone was ringing once again as it had been constantly for most of the time we were being targeted. I ignored the phone, got the paperwork as requested and was about to retreat from the room back down to the floor below when for some reason I turned back and answered the persistent ring of the phone only to find Doreen and Colin's wife on the other end of the line. Quickly messages were passed and four minds were partially put at rest!

A while after the bombardment ceased parents began to come to collect their children and when it was deemed to be safe the schools buses were dispatched to take the other pupils to their homes. We then surveyed the building. No window was left intact. One of the school buses had a badly damaged roof where masonry had fallen onto it. We realised that the structure of the fourth and fifth floors of the building were damaged but when we reached the fifth floor where the kindergarten children were taught we were presented with complete devastation. A couple of shells had hit the solid concrete roof. The tail fins of the shells were caught in the metal reinforcing rods of the ceiling and the classroom itself had taken the full force of the exploding shell. The explosion itself and the shrapnel from it had ripped the space apart and destroyed the school decks and chairs. If the class had been present I am sure not one of the children or their teachers would still have been alive. Our youngest son, then four and a half years old, would have been among them.

That afternoon Doreen and Colin's wife were safely driven out of Beirut to wait for us to collect them. For some reason, that I now cannot remember, we delayed our departure from the school and were thankful that we did as there was, after quiet for three hours, one final salvo of shells for the day that targeted the traffic at a slow moving road junction that we had to navigate on our way out of the area. When a little later than planned we went through the area there were dozens of decimated, shattered and burnt out cars in and lining the road.

That evening, safely at home with our two older boys, we just thanked the Lord for his presence, protection and help on that never to be forgotten day.

Just over two weeks later Colin gave me a letter with an Australian stamp on the envelope. "Just read that" he said. As I read I could hardly believe what I was reading. Supporters of M̲iddle E̲ast C̲hristian O̲utreach (the mission group we were part of) had prayer groups all over the world and this letter was from the leader of one such group. She wrote that the previous evening, as they met to pray as usual for Gods work in the many different countries and ministries in the Middle East that MECO was involved in, it just so happened that, they felt "a strong compulsion to pray for Lebanon and particularly for the school in East Beirut." Unusually it was an extended prayer time and lasted about two hours and they stopped when they felt it right to do so. "How are things with you all? Does this mean anything to you?"

Did it mean anything to us?

Yes it really did! Taking into account the eight hour time difference between Lebanon and Australia this group of prayers were praying for us at the exact time and length of time we were under bombardment in Beirut.

Were the events of that unusual day at school supernatural God incidents or a series of coincidents that just so happened?

25

A Gentle Whisper

The day that the school where I taught came under mortar and shell bombardment has left me with many very differing memories and thoughts. Whenever I hear or read the story about Elijah in the Bible where he hides in a cave from the sound of a hurricane wind, the shaking of an earthquake and the devastation of fire followed by the way God speaks to him in a gentle whisper that I remember one interesting incident.

When the two hour long shelling spree had ceased and I decided it was safe to move I carefully made my way downstairs and across the playground through the shattered glass and broken masonry to the underground bomb shelter to see how my four and a half year old son was coping with the terrifying incident.

He proudly told me that, although a lot of the children had been crying, he himself had not cried at all! By this time the school teachers had done a great job in comforting and calming the very young children and the atmosphere was relatively calm. Then as parents started to come to collect their children two distinct patterns of behaviour emerged. Some came in with much bluster and noise and immediately set their own children crying again as they took hold of them. Others came in gently and quietly and if their child started to cry, as many did, they sat them on their laps and quietly whispered in their ears as they rocked them in their safe arms. Soon the child was calm and at peace once again.

That day I had experienced the wind like sound of whooshing shells as they flew through the air and descended. That day I had felt the shaking of the ground and building as if in an earthquake. That day too I saw the effect of a gentle whisper on a frightened child. That day I was reminded that God comes to us in the "storms" of life, holds us in the hollow of His hand and speaks to us in that "still small voice" – that gentle whisper that brings comfort and hope in times of need.

26

The Shepherd

I taught, Science, English and Bible, in the senior section in a school for boys and girls that was located in the Ashrafiah district of East Beirut. Locals knew it as the "Evangelical School". We had total freedom to live and to teach our Christian faith. The pupil's parents, who were from the Protestant, Maronite, Catholic or Orthodox Christian communities as well as those from the Muslim and Druze communities, knew that we taught Bible lessons as part of the curriculum and held Christian assemblies every day – one for the junior pupils and one for the senior school.

At the senior assembly, typically, a couple of hymns were sung, prayers were said and a short "Christian" talk was given. At one such assembly I told the story of an old shepherd who used just five words to tell everyone who he met the most important thing in his life was that: "The Lord is my shepherd". He would emphasise this by using the four fingers and thumb of his hand to illustrate what he was saying. One hand would grasp the little finger of the other hand as he said the word "The". Moving on to the next finger came the word "Lord". The middle finger was clutched as he said "is". Then tightly holding the index finger he pronounced the word "my". Lastly he stated that the thumb stood for "shepherd". Then still keeping firmly hold of his index finger he said that the most important finger he had was the index finger and the most important thing in his life was that he knew the Lord Jesus was "my" shepherd.

Later one winter's day when tending his sheep in the hills the shepherd got caught in a snow blizzard and did not survive the night. When found it was seen that one hand was firmly holding the index finger of the other hand. Those that knew him said that not only in life but also in death he wanted people to know that the Lord was "his shepherd".

I then posed this question to the listening pupils "Can you say with certainty that Jesus is your shepherd – the one who loves you and cares for you?"

It just so happened that several weeks later a pupil reminded me of this story. Along with about ten seventeen or eighteen year old pupils we were sheltering in a short second floor corridor as the school building came under heavy shelling. The underground shelter was crammed full of children and so we had chosen the next best location where there were several walls between us and the outside of the building and any shell from above would have to come through three ceilings to reach us.

Sitting next to me on the floor was one of two blind students who attended the school. He was literally shaking with fear as he tightly held my arm as each bombardment came and subsided. Opposite me sat one of the senior girls. After several waves of shells had passed the girl asked me. "Aren't you scared sir? You don't look it."

To this I replied "I might not look it – but yes – I'm really scared!"

"Tell me - are **you** scared?" I asked her.

Vigorously nodding her head and raising her hands so I could see them she replied with the single word "but" and I saw that one hand firmly held the index finger of the other hand.

27

Doctors Shake Their Heads in Disbelief

It was said that if one could drive in Lebanon then you could drive anywhere! Normal rules of the road, for the most part, simply did not exist. This was particularly so in Beirut and its immediate surrounds. Every driver seemed to do what was right in their own eyes. Road use signage was often disregarded and all traffic lights, if they happened to be working, were completely ignored! Roundabouts were often driven over rather than be driven round if the motorist thought they could save time by doing so! No such a thing as a speed limit was adhered to! Then if traffic became slow moving it was imperative that no gap was left between cars or another car would appear from nowhere to fill the space! One could call the driving both aggressive but paradoxically it was usually also good natured at the same time. In some ways, particularly in the slower stop / start nature, of driving in the rush hour it was rather like playing a game. Who would give way first at an inter-section? Who would beat who onto a roundabout? Who would be first into the empty space just created because a vehicle in front had moved? And so it went on.

There were occasional times when small areas of Beirut became completely gridlocked because every car refused to give way to every other car and one simply did not move for prolonged periods of time. Normally in the end some cars would begin to give way to each other as they realised that without a small degree of cooperation they would be going nowhere soon. I got caught up in one such standoff where a small two lane carriageway had now become jammed with three lanes of cars because traffic at the roundabout ahead was gridlocked and at a standstill. Over the next two and a half hours my line of traffic moved only a few yards.

The roundabout, that served five roads, was in total chaos and turmoil and all the cars and trucks did not seem able to move from it such was the intransigence of the drivers. In the end heavily armed men from the local militia arrived on the scene. Several bursts of gunfire sounded out and then slowly but surely the traffic began to move once again. Militia men had stationed themselves where each of the five roads joined the roundabout and directed the vehicles one by one on their way. Any small disregarding of their instructions produced more gunfire into the air that brought the traffic back into their complete control. No one dared to ignore the directions of the gunmen.

The driving on the mountain roads and in the mountain towns was considerably more orderly, relaxed and law abiding. In the mountain town where we lived there were even several one way road systems which were actually strictly adhered to by motorists. One afternoon I was driving, accompanied by my middle son, when round a blind corner on a one way section of the road came a big car at breakneck speed. Emergency breaking and evasive action did not prevent the two cars hitting the front sides of each other. I was able to get out of the car shaken but unharmed. It was different for my son, Simon, who had not escaped unscathed. He had a huge deep cut in his leg but very much more worrying was the fact that his head had hit the windscreen and now his forehead was rapidly swelling up and had become an enormous size.

The driver of the oncoming car was uninjured and quickly took in the situation. His larger vehicle had come out of the incident relatively well and unlike my car was still drivable. Together we carried Simon and laid him down on the back seat of the other car and off we went at speed to the local medical centre that was like a mini hospital. There his leg was quickly stitched up after x-rays showed there were no broken bones. His, now huge head and skull was x-rayed but the doctor then said that he was not qualified enough to interpret the picture obtained. He was insistent that we take Simon with the x-ray down to the American University of Beirut Medical Centre for them to have a look at it and to also check him over.

By this time I had managed to contact a colleague who had collected Doreen from home and had brought her to the hospital. Together we made the journey to Beirut where several doctors examined Simon and scrutinised the head x-ray we had brought with us. After some discussion among themselves there was a nodding of heads as if in agreement. They informed us that they were not satisfied with the x-ray and would perform one themselves with what they claimed to be, and in fact was probably, better equipment. Again a group of doctors examined the new x-ray. Again there was a great deal of discussion but this time it was accompanied with much shaking of heads. Much to our consternation Simon was taken off for yet another x-ray. The three x-rays were laid out and an even larger group of doctors and radiologists intently studied them one by one.

The analysis completed we were called to hear the results of their deliberations. The lead doctor apologised for keeping us waiting but said that they wanted a third x-ray because they could find nothing untoward on the first two. He said that with such great visible trauma to the head and how it had occurred they were at first sure that a fractured skull would show up on the x-rays and could not believe they were not seeing this on the first two pictures – hence the third take. The final x-ray was also clear. "I can assure you that there has been no fracture to the skull and I am truly astonished it is intact" concluded the doctor.

We finally managed to examine the car and saw the place where Simon's head had hit and broken the windscreen. Apparently it just so happened that his forehead had hit at the point where a rolled up sun screen made of soft material was attached to the glass and so had greatly cushioned the blow. If his head had hit anywhere else the damage to his head would have been much, much more severe. As for Simon the only side effects he faced was the indignity and embarrassment of a bright purple and black heavily bruised very enlarged forehead and two magnificent black eyes! Slowly the forehead returned to its normal size and the bruising gradually changed colour as it moved down his face and eventually disappeared.

Our car was a write-off and as the driver of the other car was uninsured we had minimal recompense. On the other hand both our lives had been spared and in the days ahead we often gave thanks to God that he gave his angels charge over us "to guard us in all our ways" *(Psalm 91 v 11-12)* and that he continually looked after our going out and coming in. Of this we were very aware.

28

A Helping Hand

When asked if we would consider moving from Lebanon to Cyprus to start a MECO Video ministry and, initially also to be involved in MECO publicity both ourselves and our director thought it important that I went to Cyprus specifically to talk over more fully matters pertaining to the publicity and to look into suitable schooling for our boys.

Under normal circumstances a flight, of under half an hour, to Cyprus and the return to Lebanon would have been very easy and straightforward. But when it came to Lebanon things were often far from straightforward. As was the case in many countries in order to visit or reside in that country one needed either a visa or a residence permit. At this particular time obtaining a visa to enter Lebanon was impossible as none were being issued by the government. When it came to renewing a residence permit it seemed that the same thing was now also the case. Innumerable people were finding it impossible to get their permits renewed. Fortunately having an out of date permit did not cause any problems with the authorities as long as you remained in the country. The problem was that if you left the country it was impossible to get back in. Many who had risked leaving had found this out to their detriment. Then friends of those who had left the country found that they had to pack up the belongings of the "leavers" and either dispose of them or try to freight them out of the country.

At that time my residence permit had expired and unless I could guarantee that I could re-enter the country I did not want to visit Cyprus for that all important fact finding trip. I was well aware that over the past few months numerous friends had tried multiple times to renew their permits. Weekly we were asked to pray that various people would be able to obtain that coveted document. Although it was actually a residence permit many of us only saw it as a travel permit! Those individuals whose permits had expired and who had to leave the country for various reasons did not manage to return and so found that one chapter of their lives had regretfully ended unexpectedly.

Now I found myself in the position where I really, really needed to have a valid, up to date, residency card.

So early one morning I joined a long queue of foreigners from many different countries outside the building in Beirut where applications for residence permits were processed. I had put together all the necessary documents and photographs that were needed and just hoped and prayed that I would actually be able to get into the relevant office to see if I could even get to lodge the application. Most people were finding that the officials on taking a first look at the applications rejected them, often without explanation. If the paperwork was accepted, and that hardly ever happened, the applicant was asked to return in a week's time to see if residency had indeed been granted. Then when they returned it was only to be told that the application had failed. For weeks we had not heard of anyone who had succeeded.

The waiting crowd was patrolled by police and soldiers to stop people from queue jumping and moved forward very, very slowly. It was a known fact that it could take several attempts to even enter the office building. I had joined the queue before the offices were opened and there was just half an hour left before they were due to close. Suddenly a very grand looking military officer, resplendent in a colourful, much decorated uniform was strolling down the waiting column. When he reached me he stopped and in perfect English said "I think it is too late for you to get in today. Why not come back and try again tomorrow?" Without really thinking I replied that it was very important that I get the required permit and as there was so little time till closing time I would wait with the hope of gaining entry. With a smile and an "As you wish" he turned and strode back into the building. Then even more near closing time the officer appeared at the door and catching my eye beckoned me forward and took me into the building and straight to the processing office where, out of my hearing, he said something to the desk clerk. When I handed over my papers I was elated that after having looked them over the clerk filed them and told me to come back next week. Stage one completed – thank you Lord. I looked for the officer to thank him for his help but he was nowhere to be found inside or outside the offices.

A week later I was queueing again. After many weeks of other people being unsuccessful would I be the first to actually come away with a valid permit? Would the prayers of many be answered? Again, after a long wait in the hot sun, I saw the officer from the previous week standing in the doorway. This time he did not venture out but just stood there. Thinking that there was nothing to lose I left the queue and greeted the man, thanked him for his help the previous week and turned to return to my place in the queue. As I did so he said "Go on in and up to the office." When in the actual office, as several others were being dealt before my turn came, I noticed that the officer was standing at the back of the room. When finally at the counter the clerk already had my file to hand and without further ado passed me a new residence permit. Thank you Lord. I would soon be on my way to Cyprus safe in the knowledge that I would be able to return to the family in Lebanon.

Once again I tried to find the officer to thank him for his help but to no avail and furthermore, it just so happened that when questioned, none of the other office officials could tell me who he actually was or why he was there!

Did I have supernatural help? Was my, seemingly unidentifiable, helping officer a descriptive or literal angel?

29

The Bionic Ear

That night the rains were torrential. Even if we found the "Bionic Ear" it would surely be unusable, drowned by the rains or trodden under foot and shattered. We looked at each other with heavy hearts and a feeling of hopelessness.

It all began when our youngest son was eighteen months old. He was a beautiful and happy child, very contented and full of love. It was late in the evening and he hadn't long been asleep when he began to cry. It was not just an ordinary cry but an agonized shrill of pain. As he lay on my lap screaming to the point of breathlessness, his body became rigid, burning with a high fever. We had no telephone, no car, and the hospital was a fair distance away. My husband rushed and fetched a near neighbour who happened to be an English doctor. He came and did the usual thing like taking the temperature and feeling the pulse, but he couldn't ease the agony of our son.

There we were three adults sitting around a screaming baby, feeling totally helpless and desperately seeking to bring him comfort but not knowing how. "Lord, what is going on? Lord, please help"! Our only option was to begin piercing the heavens with our prayer sirens, anxiously pulling the Lord's hand of mercy to place on our little child. Our son screamed and we prayed. The louder the baby cried the more concentrated became our pleading. "Lord, have mercy. Lord, heal. Lord, stop whatever is harming this child. Lord, save his life". We were all Christians, serving the Lord in full time ministry, living in a foreign country and studying the language and culture in order to serve the people whom the Lord had called us to live amongst.

After a while his cries ceased and he fell into a fitful exhausted sleep. In the morning one side of his body appeared to be slightly paralysed, so we took him to see a child specialist, who, after examining him, suggested that he might have a broken collarbone. We then went elsewhere for an X ray and the collarbone showed up fine. We consulted another specialist who was equally mystified by the condition. As our son continued to be slightly paralysed on one side we contacted a third child specialist who was unable to diagnose his condition. Over the next few weeks however, the paralysis diminished until we forgot all about the distressing incident.

Over the course of the next two years it became apparent that our son had quite a hearing loss. Three years later we returned home to the U.K. Doctors probed our son's medical history, finally diagnosing him as having contracted encephalitis, which caused him partial hearing loss and meant he needed the help of a hearing aid. They also added that it was a miracle he was still alive and not brain damaged!

I grieved deeply for the partial hearing loss in my little son. I became angry and resentful. "Lord, you called us to serve you abroad so why did you let our child go through such an ordeal?" A fierce battle raged within me. At times it burned very deeply and seemed almost unconquerable. Yet on the other hand, I did praise the Lord, I was grateful to Him, I was aware of our son's miraculous recovery, but it still hurt! We spent a little time in the U.K. and were now back in the Middle East again. Hearing aids were not so familiar where we lived. The people had a deep seated, instinctive fear of any minor disability, so how were we to introduce the little aid to the children and the staff of his school? Action Man was a favourite toy with the children at that time, and the Bionic Man was a regular T.V. programme, hence the introduction of the hearing aid as the "Bionic Ear" seemed very appropriate. Before many days mums were questioning me about the bionic ear as their children were asking to wear them! To this day it is still referred to as his "Bionics".

The day before the torrential rains, he returned home from school, which was just down the road from where we lived and realized that his Bionic ear was missing! We hurriedly retraced our steps examining every place along the roadside where it might have fallen. Entering the school playground we alerted the caretaker and the staff, then an intensive hunt began. Unfortunately it was not found. After my husband returned from work he too went looking but returned sad faced. We prayed asking the Lord's protection over the little instrument and went to bed having done all in our power. That night the heavens opened, pouring rain soaked the earth, causing the hilly roads to become like running rivers. Early that wet morning my husband retraced his steps hoping for a sight of the gadget even if it was destroyed by the rains. Again he returned without finding it.

Around mid-morning the telephone rang. It was the school secretary asking me to go and confirm if what they had found was the "Bionic". My feet hardly touched the ground as I sped to the school and sure enough our lost treasure was found!

It had lain safely all night in the centre of the school incinerator! Every evening after lessons, the caretaker would sweep the school playground and place the rubbish in the incinerator ready for burning the next morning. That morning it just so happened that the fire refused to burn. He tried lighting the incinerator for a second and third time but the fire would not start. He then took his rake and parted the rubbish, lying happily among the leaves and empty packets of crisps was our precious bionic ear, totally dry and very functional having been well protected from the previous night's downpour. My heart bubbled with sheer joy and exhilaration. "Lord", I shouted inwardly "thank you, thank you, thank you". I was lost for words but utterly grateful. "Somebody's looking after you", said the caretaker.

We were living in a country riddled by a tumultuous civil war. That incident was very meaningful. It brought a renewed sense of the Lord's peace and presence to us. If the Lord could take care of that little "Bionic Ear" and protect it from ruin how much more was he protecting and caring for our family amid the fighting, shooting and shelling. "Do not be of little faith". "I am with you always". Standing on the Lords Promises kept our feet firm and our faith sure.

Many years have passed since that incident. The little boy has grown, he is now a graduate with a responsible job, and we are still rejoicing in the Lord's goodness for our family.

"Fear Not I AM with you, be not dismayed for I AM your God. I WILL strengthen you and help you ". *Isaiah 41 v10*

What a promise!

Written by Doreen Holmes and published in the Christian Herald on 3rd February 2001.

30

Target Practice

In Lebanon a civil war, starting in 1975, went on till 1990. The result was that at times there was very heavy fighting of one kind or another while at other times relative peace was the order of the day although one was well aware that at any time, for any little reason, things could erupt once again.

Often a new eruption of fighting would consist of an exchange of mortar and tank shells as well as small arms fire. Sometimes these appeared to be at random but at other times it became evident that certain specific areas or buildings were being targeted. These shelling exchanges sometimes only lasted for short spells of time but caused havoc and devastation to those targeted and instilled fear in the wider civilian population.

There were quite a number of different political groups and each had its own fighters or militia force. Each area of the country was controlled by one militia or another who fiercely guarded their own "territory". To this mix of numerous Lebanese militias was added the Syrian army that had entered the country as a peace keeping force in 1976 but soon became viewed by many as an occupying army. Then in 1982 Israeli forces occupied the south of the country and surrounded and laid siege to Beirut from the mountains surrounding the city and from the Christian enclave north of Beirut. Between 1982 and 1984 to this mix were added a Multinational Force of "peacekeepers" comprised of troops from the USA, France, Italy and the United Kingdom who were deployed mainly in Beirut and its immediate environs. Meanwhile in southern Lebanon there was a contingent of Fijian soldiers acting under the flag of a United Nations Peacekeeping Force.

However when there was no fighting life went on in a very normal way with one usually being able to travel between the areas that had been at odds with each other with no problems at all. All the roads into each "territory" had checkpoints guarding them. Sometimes you could just slow down and be waved through them in your car but, more often than not, you had to stop and have your papers and vehicle checked. Often they would also ask you where you going and why. Sometimes it was quite intimidating and aggressive but frequently, particularly if it was a quiet road, those manning the checkpoint would chat with you amicably.

Many people had second homes in the mountains of Lebanon that they would normally only use during the hot summer months as they were deemed too cold to use in winter. However with the advent of the civil war many people had to retreat to the mountains all year round in the hope of avoiding the shelling that was mainly targeted at the cities and towns.

Nevertheless there were occasions when shelling took place in the mountains. There was one place in the mountains of the Christian area where a number of true Christian believers had their summer houses and there was also one tall block of apartments that were the homes of several related families. From a distance this solitary apartment block was rather prominent and stood out on the wooded hillside. One day, quite randomly and without warning, tank and mortar rounds were fired into the "Christian" area by the Syrian army "peacekeepers". This went on, on and off, for about two hours. The apartment block, at the time, was very crowded with families, as many had come to the mountains for refuge from the fighting in Beirut. As so often happens in such situations the people were earnestly praying for safety as the shells landed all around them. Thankfully no one was injured as most of shells missed the buildings and fell into the surrounding wooded area.

When news of this incident became known, a friend of ours living in Beirut, decided to go up into the mountains to check that his many friends were alright. As he approached and got his first glimpse of his friend's apartment block he was pulled over to be checked at a Syrian army roadblock. Papers were duly scrutinised, car bonnet and boot opened and searched for weapons and my friend was asked where he was going. So he pointed up into the distance at the single apartment block on the wooded hillside in the distance. A strange look came on the soldier's face and he said "Who lives there? They are very lucky." "Yes", replied my friend, "it has really beautiful views". "I did not mean the views" answered the soldier in a rather offhand way, "we've just used that building for target practice but we couldn't seem to be able to hit it".

Was that a supernatural God incident or just a lucky coincident as the soldier at the checkpoint said?

31

Peace in the Mountains – But War in the City

Lebanon was once under the colonial rule of France who designed the government of the country to provide political representation for all the religious groups. The three largest groups being Christian Maronites, Sunni Muslims and Shiite Muslims. The president must always be a Christian, the prime minister a Sunni Muslim and the speaker of parliament a Shia Muslim. Seats in parliament, government posts and public-sector positions were also divided among these three groups in a similar way. To complicate the matter further these three broad groupings between them were together made up of some eighteen recognised religious sects.

Then there were further sub groups to be found within all these eighteen sects. At times during the civil war in Lebanon there were said to be upwards of sixty to seventy factions and each of the factions had its own fighters or militia. The bigger groups in fact had mini armies and carved out their own territories and sought to control them by manning checkpoints or roadblocks on the roads leading into and out of their areas or enclaves. Depending how belligerent or militant any group was at any given time determined whether one travelled from one area of the country to another. There were times when it was reasonable and safe to travel quite widely and go through enclaves controlled by many different groups but at other times it was only sensible to make short journeys even if staying in the enclave controlled by the militia in whose area one lived. Then there were times that it was not sensible to go out at all!

At various times some militias made alliances with other militias. So one Christian militia might agree to form an alliance with another Christian militia or even with one of the Muslim militias or indeed any number of militias might align themselves with each other. The only problem was that these alliances could, and indeed frequently did, change overnight. Friends one day could be the enemy the next day. Friends one day could be killing each other the next day. There was always rapid and constant change. Fortunately outbreaks of violence between different groups lasted, mostly, for only very short periods of time and after a few days things would return to what was deemed as normal. However in times of unrest it felt that one was imprisoned in a very small area of the country and it could drain the spirit.

It just so happened that there was one particular time, however, when the situation in the country had remained very volatile for quite a number of weeks and we all felt "trapped" in our enclave and longed to get out into the countryside or go up into the high mountains for some relaxation. We had become friends with another family, new to the country, who "were going mad" with not being able to travel more than a few miles from home because of the situation. One day, after consultations with several other friends, as the situation appeared to have calmed down our two families decided to get in our cars and head into the high pine and cedar tree laden mountain slopes for a picnic and to enjoy some freedom.

As we drove down to the outskirts of Beirut to pick up the main highway leading up into the mountains we noted that there were more checkpoints and that they were much more thorough than usual. But as there were other vehicles on the roads we were not unduly concerned. When far away from Beirut we left the main Beirut to Damascus highway and travelled along some very minor roads that led deep into the upper reaches of the mountains. When we finally arrived at our destination, we found a beautiful lonely spot among the cedar trees and had a wonderful few hours breathing in the fresh mountain air. Together we marvelled at and revelled in the beauty of God's creation. As we walked, talked, enjoyed the pine scented air and the freedom afforded by the mountains we heard in the distance the constant boom of explosions. We were not unduly concerned by this as we concluded that we were hearing the long ongoing fighting that was taking place at that time in the Beqaa valley just over the other side of the mountain from where we were picnicking. We did not even consider that it might be coming from the Beirut area.

Time came for us to return home and as we exited the small mountain roads and joined the main highway going down to Beirut we noticed with some growing concern that the nearer we got to the outskirts of Beirut the less the traffic became until we seemed to be the only cars on the road. We came to a roadblock and had to stop and were told by the soldiers manning it that it was far too dangerous to continue down into Beirut. When we told them that our destination was not in the centre of Beirut but in the foothills above they opened the barriers and sent us on our way with the words "Hurry", Hurry" "Hurry" ringing in our ears. Travelling at top speed on completely empty roads we soon arrived at our friend's home safe and sound. Neighbours rushed out to enquire if we were alright and asked us if we had been caught up in the fighting of the day. We assured them that no fighting had affected us the whole day and that our carefree day in the mountains had been a real tonic.

They told us they had been praying all day that we would be safe as shortly after we had set out fighting had broken out in and between the areas that we had to drive through to get into the mountains and had only stopped a short while before we got home. While we enjoyed the open freedom of the mountains they had spent the day in their "safe" rooms.

Was that day of much needed physical, mental and spiritual refreshment a day long God incident?

32

Peace Keepers

In the rear view mirror of the car as I drove in downtown Beirut I could see that there was an unusual movement in the flow of the very slowly moving line of traffic. It seemed that the vehicles were moving over toward the sides of the road causing a gap to open up in the usually dense flow of traffic. Generally any small gap in the traffic would soon be filled, but not on this occasion. Then the reason became evident. A very small armoured ferret scout car was forcing its way slowly through the traffic and fluttering at the top of its long radio antenna was a union jack flag. Soldiers of the British contingent of the Multinational Force of peacekeepers had arrived. They consisted of a squadron of eighty men from the 1st Queen's Dragoon Guards with their miniscule fighting vehicles. Nine months later they were to be replaced with a one hundred and fifteen strong unit from the 16th/5th Royal Lancers. At that time they probably doubled the number of British citizens in Lebanon.

A young British colleague managed to made contact with them and obtained an invite to bring the few British children that he knew were still in Lebanon to visit their base on the outskirts of Beirut. The children had the time of their lives climbing in and out of various military vehicles and looking at all the weaponry and equipment. The rides in the ferret scout cars were probably the highlight of their visit. The children loved the experience and I think the soldiers enjoyed it even more. It was a tense deployment for these soldiers who, when not out on patrol, were not allowed to leave the base. Also they were regularly shot at and on many occasions had to intervene and broker a peace, in the midst of crossfire, between various armed factions that had fallen out with each other. All of this was forgotten for a time as they looked after the children.

To try to give some soldiers a break from the monotony of base life and to thank them for the great time they had given our boys when they visited their base Doreen decided to invite some of the soldiers to our home in the mountains for a meal. So it was that special permission was granted by the base commander for a group of twenty men to visit us. On the way they would see something of the beauty of the mountains of Lebanon rather than the daily sight of destruction and disorder in built-up Beirut itself. An officer volunteered, or being the army was possibly volunteered, to accompany the soldiers and also to liaise with me about the details of their afternoon and evening out as civilians.

The appointed day arrived and I left Doreen at home busy preparing a whole variety of different dishes in great quantities determined, as usual, that no one would go away hungry! As normal I was in school that day and around one o'clock was expecting a phone call from the organising officer telling us when they were about to leave. The phone duly rang and the officer told me that they were just about to be on their way but he then apologised, broke off from what he was saying and asked me to hang on a moment. A few seconds later he came on the line again and said "I don't know how to say this but we will have to cancel our visit. I've no idea what's going on but we have just this very minute been placed on high alert and cannot leave the base." While he was speaking I heard some talking in the background and he then went on to say "They've blown up the American embassy." It turned out that at one o'clock a suicide car bomber had detonated a device that demolished the front of the multi-storey embassy building killing sixty three people.

So it was that the soldiers did not get their trip out and a good home cooked English meal. Doreen's, ever resourceful, quick thinking though meant the prepared food did not go to waste. She rounded up nearby colleagues, friends and neighbours and together we enjoyed a great time and a great meal.

33

A Man From Cana in Galilee

The large church in Beirut was packed with a sombre crowd of people. Outside many more were clustered in small groups quietly talking with one another or silently waiting around for the service inside the church to end so that they could accompany the remains of the man in the coffin to his final earthly resting place. The man whose life we were remembering and giving thanks to God for was a local Palestinian Christian teacher.

When first introduced to Jamil one of the first things he wanted me to know was that he was from Cana in Galilee. He was very proud of the fact that he had been born in the town where Jesus performed his first miracle of turning water into wine. He had spent the first few years of his life there until devastating turmoil broke out when the state of Israel was founded. Then his immediate Palestinian family were forced to leave their home and they fled to Lebanon as refugees. Although refugees the family worked hard to ensure that Jamil had a good education that enabled him to train as a teacher, leave refugee status behind and become integrated into Lebanese society. Although they wished that they could do so the family were never permitted to return to their old family home in Cana. However Jamil told me that he still had relatives in Cana and hoped and prayed that one day he would be able to visit them.

He came from a nominal Christian family but as a result of the Christian teaching that he heard in the school assemblies and saw demonstrated in the lives of true followers of Christ he came to know Jesus as his Saviour and friend. From that time on he had an overwhelming desire to tell others of his faith in God and never missed an opportunity to do so. He did this fearlessly and enthusiastically and did not differentiate between the nominal Christian population and those that counted themselves Muslims. In school, in shared service taxis, in shops and when just out and about he made, and never missed, opportunities to tell others about Jesus.

A small group of foreign Christian teachers along with a few local teachers used to meet each week to pray together. It was at these times that one really got to know him. His tremendous desire to visit his birth place, his desire to find a wife and get married, his distress that he was not as "good" a Christian as he wanted to be, his sense of his own sinfulness and his desire to become more like Jesus. He shared personal things that he wanted us to pray for, such as his health or a difficult pupil or class in school. He would tell us about the conversations that he had had with others about his faith and those who he was expecting to talk with.

Early in the civil war a Christian militia, located in southern Lebanon next to the Israeli border, became allies of the Israelis. This enabled some Lebanese citizens to cross the border freely to visit Israel. One prayer time Jamil excitedly asked us to pray that an application he had made to visit Cana would be granted by the authorities involved. A short time later he had the permit, travelled to Cana and as he put it had the joy of not only meeting many relatives he had not seen for many years but also of speaking about his faith in the local church and in the homes of his relatives.

Another prayer time he shared the fact that later in the week he was meeting up with a couple of Muslims who wanted to know more about Jesus. He asked us to pray that he would have special wisdom and courage as he spoke with them.

That was the last time I saw him.

On Sunday he was not in church and could not be found at home. He had simply vanished without trace. A few days later his headless body was found. He had been brutally murdered with a "necklace bomb".

The Christian community were in no doubt that he had been martyred for his faith in Jesus. The details of his abduction and murder never came to light. Were those two enquirers he had asked us to pray for genuine? Had other militants found out they were talking together and then acted in hatred? We can only speculate.

When the arrangements were made for his funeral and burial it somehow felt fitting that, like Jesus, he was to be put into a new "borrowed" family tomb owned by a close Palestinian friend and colleague who also arranged the funeral service.

As Jamil's funeral service was coming to an end and his coffin was being carried from the church those gathered there sung, with much feeling, a hymn in Arabic that summed up his trust and faith in God.

> "I have decided to follow Jesus; No turning back, no turning back.
> The world behind me, the cross before me;
> No turning back, no turning back.
> Though none go with me, still I will follow;
> No turning back, no turning back.
> My cross I'll carry, till I see Jesus; No turning back, no turning back.
> Will you decide now to follow Jesus? No turning back, no turning back."

Jamil had fearlessly carried high the cross of Jesus till he met Him in heaven but if he had still been alive he would have been asking all he met:

"Will you decide now to follow Jesus?" It is a question we all should consider and honestly answer.

34

Memories of Air Travel

Over the years I spent quite a lot of time in various airports and on various aircraft. As I think back I remember with mixed emotions some of the things I saw and some of the things I experienced. Below are a few of the more memorable ones.

One of the short haul aircraft in use between Cyprus, Lebanon, Syria, Egypt and Jordan was the small, eighty seater, British Aircraft Corporation One-Eleven aircraft. I do not know if its small size made it more prone to be affected by the forces of nature such as wind but it is for this that I remember it. The runway at Larnaca airport was known to be susceptible to cross winds and on one occasion a very strong gust caught my aircraft moments before landing, the plane tilted sideways at an alarming angle, and at that point the engines roared with a burst of power as the pilot aborted the landing and flew round for a second attempt. Doreen, with our boys, had been watching as the plane came over the end of the runway and were horrifyingly alarmed as they saw one wing tip, seemingly inches from ploughing into the runway. Much urgent prayer was answered as the second effort to land was safely accomplished.

On another occasion a similar aircraft took off from Larnaca straight into a storm. Rain was pelting down, low clouds were swirling around and the wind was blowing in strong gusts. As for the aircraft itself - it seemed as if it was being tossed around the sky like a ship on a stormy sea! One got the tangible sense that the pilot really was flying and controlling the speed and direction of the aircraft. It appeared that he was trying to fly it round or away from some of the churning clouds that we were flying amongst. The engines in turn roared and then became almost silent again as the plane sped up and slowed down. Passengers were screaming and one of the flight attendants moved down the aisle on her knees holding firmly on to each row of seats that she passed. This was in order to administer first aid to a passenger who it was feared was suffering a heart attack. Slowly the assault of the storm on the plane diminished and a thankful calm descended on the passengers grateful to be able to arrive alive at their destination. I must admit that after that scary incident on this occasion if I could have returned home to Cyprus overland I would have done so but alas that was impossible to do!

I was visiting Jordan and booked a flight to return home to Cyprus. As it took just over an hour to fly between the two countries I looked forward to being back home soon. On arrival at the airport I found out that my journey was going to be considerably longer as the aircraft had been rescheduled to go via Damascus in Syria instead of being the usual direct flight. I was told the reason for the unexpected change was that the aircraft was being repositioned for use on other routes. Seeing how many people were checking in I realised that it would be a full aircraft. Indeed it was and very unusually for this route a large three engine Lockheed TriStar plane was being used. This type of aircraft was one of the biggest available at that time and could carry almost four hundred passengers and crew. The plane I boarded that day was packed and I do not think that there were any spare seats. The short, less than a half hour flight to Damascus, was soon completed and to my amazement virtually all the passengers disembarked. When we took off again there were only three passengers left on board the massive aircraft along with many cabin crew. The onward hour long flight to Larnaca was taken up with snacks, drinks and chatting with the cabin staff who themselves were enjoying this, now stress free, journey. They told us that after disembarking us few remaining passengers in Cyprus they were taking the, now passenger free, plane back to the UK and were, like us, looking forward to getting home to their families.

Often for friends I carried letters and small items to Egypt to ensure they arrived quickly at their destination so often my baggage was overweight. By this time those on the check in desk had got to recognise "Mr David" and so overlooked the extra pounds. One morning after checking in as I waited for the flight to be called a loudspeaker announcement was made, "Could Mr David please return to the check in desk." I duly complied and was then taken to where the baggage was x-rayed before going out to be loaded onto the aircraft. On a bench was a solidary suitcase – my suitcase. "What have you got in there?" enquired a worried looking official. "Would you be willing to open it?" "Of course I will. I will show you" I replied advancing towards the case. As I moved forward others in the room moved back and it then dawned on me what all the fuss was about. They were worried that I was carrying a bomb! The case was opened, the contents were shown and the previously cowering baggage handlers were soon gathered round laughing and patting me on the back. It just so happened that packed in the case were twenty four, large cigarette size, boxes. Attached to each box and wrapped around each of them were wires. At that time there were no small hearing aids that could be discretely hidden behind or in the ear but the aids were large units that were held in shirt pockets or clipped onto clothes. Wires ran from the small box unit to the earpiece. My suspect package consisted of hearing aids that I was going to deliver, for a friend, to a centre for the deaf in Cairo. I could see why they thought, on x-raying my suitcase, that it might contain a bomb.

Rumour had it that some airlines were beginning to secretly put armed sky or air marshals onto their aircraft to deal with any terrorist attack or attempted hijacking that might occur. Over a short period of time I had used one particular airline for a number of flights and realised that there was one man that I had seen on every flight. As I was sure he was not following me I concluded that he must be one of the rumoured secret security guards. His action at Beirut airport proved I was correct when, as the only non-Arab on that particular flight, he picked me out at the aircraft gate from the other passengers and with the words, "Come with me, you must keep safe", he hurriedly escorted me onto the waiting plane. This came after being moved to the front of the check in queue and then quickly ushered through security, again at the front of the waiting queue. I was very fortunate to have this special treatment as it was at the time when foreigners were being abducted and held hostage in the country.

As I look back I can recall many, many such similar incidents when people unknown to me, took it upon themselves to make sure that I was kept safe in a whole range of particularly difficult situations and places.

35

A Significant Gift

Because we could no longer educate our children in Lebanon it became increasingly apparent that we could not live or work there any longer. Added to this the fact that the British government, several months before, had requested that all UK subjects leave the country we thought that perhaps our time in the Middle East was coming to an end and that a return to England was imminent. However our director had other ideas and we were asked to move to Cyprus in order to look into the possible use of Christian videos in Arabic. This we did.

When research had been carried out it became very apparent that, save for one sub-titled film, there were in fact no other Christian films or Christian teaching material available in Arabic on video at that time. The next question posed was – "how could MECO become involved in the production and use of this new medium of communication?" So a possible plan of action was drawn up. Firstly we could seek to sub-title in Arabic Christian films made in USA and U.K. Secondly we could film series of Christian teachings in Arabic. Along with this we would fully voice dub films into Arabic. Then original films in Arabic could be produced. It became very clear that if MECO were to pursue this area of work then it would involve huge (for MECO) sums of money. However our International Council, praying that God would supply the necessary money if this work was to go ahead agreed that we should start to implement our plan of action if I felt it was a viable and sensible proposition when I had obtained specific costings for the various projected projects.

More detailed research and enquiries were initiated. We awaited a reply from a Christian film maker in USA asking what payment would be required in order to have their permission to subtitle twelve of their films in Arabic. At the same time I went to Egypt to find out the costs of having the films subtitled in a studio in Cairo.

As I was on the plane returning to Cyprus I mulled over the fact that decision time had come as to whether MECO should proceed with a video ministry. It just so happened that at that time we only had the sum of about $100 in the video account and the cost of the proposed subtitling project would amount to $10,000 plus the unknown cost of the USA sourced films and their use. It seemed like an unsurmountable mountain was in our path but I became convinced that it was now or never for MECO to embark on a video ministry and by the time the plane landed my mind was made up that we should proceed, in faith, on at least the subtitling project. We would then proceed with the other items on the action plan step by step as the Lord provided the expertise and the necessary finance.

Because it was an early morning flight from Cairo I was back in the office in the afternoon to catch up with work that had accumulated while I had been away. Thumbing through the post I found an envelope with USA stamps and was delighted that it was the reply I was waiting for from the USA Christian film production company. They stated that they were thrilled that we wanted to subtitle their films and their board had decided that we could have and use the films at no cost to ourselves. They just requested that we make a short annual report as to the sale and use of the films. Thank you Lord – that was one hurdle over for this first video project. Now we just needed a mere 10,000 USA dollars – the equivalent of approximately $40,000- $50,000 today.

I had hardly got over the exciting news I had just received when our treasurer came over from an office in another building. He said that he had just heard that I was back from Cairo and wanted to bring me some good news. A gift had just been received by MECO specifically stating that it was for our proposed video ministry. It amounted to a few dollars short of $10,000.

A recognition that the Lord's hand was on our projected ministry came to me in an even greater way and I also felt that it showed that the Lord had a real sense of humour when I found out the source of the necessary funds. The money had been given by an expatriate group of Christians, meeting week by week to worship, in a country where there were no church buildings and the possession of a Bible, by a local person, was not even allowed. This was their Easter offering and because the money had to come to us via the USA it had taken a couple of months to reach us – on just the right day.

What a day.

Although no money was yet to hand a positive decision had been made to progress a video ministry.

Permission for the free use of films was granted by the copyright owners.

One cheque for all the money needed for the first project was received - and that from the very heart of the Arab world!

A series of supernatural God incidents or just many coincidents?

36

"Let Us Pray"

In the early 1980's home video machines were just beginning to be used in England and video cassette hire shops were few and far between. In the Middle East however shops hiring out video cassettes were to be found everywhere and machines to play them were to be found in many homes and other places where people met together – sometimes in the most unusual of places such as tented homes in the desert.

MECO had seen the possibility of using this medium for Christian teaching and evangelism and were beginning to become actively involved in providing such material in Arabic.

We very much led the field in this and became the people that were in great demand by personnel in other foreign Christian groups working among Arabic speaking people worldwide and also by local Christian groups.

One such group were Coptic Orthodox Church lay priests living and working in the city of Assiut a six hour journey south by express train from Cairo.

I was told that one of the lay priests had lobbied his bishop for many months to obtain permission to meet up with and talk to me about the video work and productions we were involved in.

It just so happened that in time permission was granted and a meeting was set up and held in the Orthodox Church complex. It was just great to meet up with a godly young man who, having trained as a doctor, believed that God had now called him into the ministry of the church. We spoke at length about how we could be of help to each other in seeking to use video in our outreach work of the gospel.

As we concluded our deliberations in his very large office the priest said "Let us pray together brother David". I was delighted to agree to his request. Immediately he turned off the main lighting in the room and turned on a spotlight that lit up a picture of Christ on the cross that was set high up in the corner of the room. He then led off our prayer time together with, not a liturgical prayer, but a beautiful spontaneous informal prayer. The room was filled with the presence of the Lord.

Later, as I thought about this time of prayer, I smiled to myself as I wondered what my evangelical Christians supporters in England would have made of it. At that time evangelicals viewed with great suspicion anyone not of their persuasion. But then my new priest friend had to get permission from his Bishop to speak to this evangelical heretic!

Then one day, months later, my priest friend with tongue in cheek remarked that he did not know what the world was coming to as the Orthodox Church that had remained true to the faith since the time of Christ was now turning to these new upstart evangelicals to help them in the spreading of the faith.

37

Fasting and prayer

Much of the video work that I was doing involved Egypt and Egyptian Christians in one way or another. Quick communication was always a problem. Internet, email, and mobile phone means of communications did not yet exist and, for the most part, land line telephone links, especially internationally, could not be relied on even if they theoretically existed.

Usually letter post would eventually get to its destination but anything larger than a letter could not be guaranteed to arrive intact. So fellow Christian travellers would often hand carry items for each other between various countries to ensure important or sensitive mail arrived at its destination. Between Cyprus and Egypt it worked very well as most weeks there were travellers going to and fro.

At one point I was awaiting an important, much needed, small package from Cairo but unusually there were no travellers scheduled for several weeks. I decided to wait a few days in case that changed but reached the point where I could wait no longer so went out and purchased my air ticket to fly to Cairo in two days-time to collect the package. I would then have to wait in Cairo another two days in order to get the next flight back to Cyprus.

At that time MECO had no workers in Cairo that I could stay with as they were all employed much further south - a full half days train travel away. When I arrived mid-morning in Cairo I made my way directly to a hotel I sometimes stayed in to drop off my bags before going off to complete the business I had come to do in the afternoon.

When entering the hotel lobby there was mutual surprise when I came face to face with a MECO colleague. She was hurrying to catch a train back to her place of work six hours south of Cairo. She asked if I was going to come south as well but I said I would not have time on this occasion as I was going back to Cyprus the day after next. She made a passing comment that it was a pity as there was another group of Egyptian Christians that wanted to meet up with me. I told her that I would make sure that the next time I came to Egypt I would journey south to meet them. Then off she went to catch her train and off I went to complete my business.

Business completed I looked forward to the next day being free to do some sightseeing and photography in the souks of Cairo. It turned out to be a very good day and I got some excellent photos particularly as a friendly policeman joined himself to me and "helped" pave the way for me take the scenes I wanted to capture on film. I was also able to get some shots that were only possible because of his "perceived minder" presence!

Arriving back at the hotel the receptionist said that an Egyptian man had kept phoning up wanting to speak to me. I was a little mystified as I had no idea who could be trying to contact me. A little later I was called down to the reception to take a call. "Is that brother David who has videos?" said the voice over the line. When I replied in the affirmative the voice continued "Praise the Lord. You are the answer to our prayers. Can I come to your hotel now and speak to you?"

A little later we met up and I got answers to questions that had been going through my mind after his phone call. He was the representative of a group of Christians living in Assiut, a six hour journey south of Cairo. His group wanted to use our video productions and wanted to talk to me – it must be the same group my colleague had mentioned the day before.

My new friend said that four days ago his group had met and agreed to fast and pray together until such time as they were able to meet up with me – it just so happened that it was the same day I decided I could wait no longer and bought my air ticket. Then yesterday he said that he had, by accident, met my colleague in the street as she made her way home from the train station in Assiut. When she mentioned to him that she had just seen me in Cairo he asked if I was coming south. No - she informed him and also the fact that I was returning to Cyprus the day after next. Having ascertained where I was staying he had then caught the night train to Cairo in the hope that he could meet me before I left the city. So here we were now meeting. He and his group's prayers had been quickly answered – his group could now break their fast and turn their prayers to other matters!

Were they supernatural God directed incidents or just a series of coincidents that just so happened to make our meeting possible?

38

First Class Travel

Before so many people had got used to travelling all over the world on holiday a number of people said to me that it must have been great to travel such a lot by plane. If truth be told air travel became simply a means to an end and not something to delight in. Between some Middle East countries one would have to allow a whole day for a half hour or forty five minute flight. There was travel to the airport to be there at least two hours before the flight. Then more often than not the flight was delayed. After the flight it could take two or three hours, particularly in Cairo airport to get through immigration and customs inspection, before, an often hair raising taxi or bus ride to your destination.

Then on longer distances I always wondered if I would make the connecting flight. On one such occasion I was returning to England from Cyprus and the most cost effective way of doing this was to fly into Amsterdam, Schiphol airport and catch a connecting flight to London, Heathrow or Gatwick. On this occasion we were late taking off from Larnaca airport in Cyprus but I and some others were told that we should still make the connecting flight to London. Into Schiphol we came - but still late. Now at that time, if you had several "legs" to your flight travel, you had to go to the transit desk at the next airport along the way. This was to check in to the next leg of your journey and obtain another boarding pass for this new leg of your journey. So I arrived at a crowded transit desk and joined the queue behind a person dressed like a tourist who had been on my flight from Cyprus and was hoping to make the same connecting flight to Heathrow as I hoped to travel on. After he had presented himself at the desk I heard him being told that he was too late to make the connection and was put on a flight to London leaving three hours later. Thinking that I would also be put on the later flight I was a little concerned that there was no way that I could contact my father and mother who were due to meet me at Heathrow meaning that they would have a long tiring wait into the night. (Remember – forty years ago there was no mobile phone or instant internet communication.) Once at the transit desk the man behind the counter, to my amazement said "If you really hurry sir, you can just make your flight. I've upgraded you to first class". Why did he do this? Was it because I was wearing a suit and was carrying a brief case? I made the flight and enjoyed the luxury on this last leg of my journey.

A supernatural God incident or just a coincident?

39

Unexpected Exhibitions

We told people, if asked, that springtime was the best time to visit any of the countries that we lived in during our time in the Middle East. In spring it was possible to enjoy being out in the sun without it becoming too hot to enjoy, even at its hottest. Another reason for a visit at that time was that the countryside was carpeted with the flowers of spring. Swathes of every shade of red, blue, yellow, purple and white covered the hills and valleys replacing the winter drabness and bringing life to the landscape.

During one of our trips into the countryside the boys joined their mother in picking a few of the tiny brightest blooms. When we got home Doreen decided to preserve them. So she placed some between the pages of books and piled other books on top of them. Others she simply placed between sheets of paper and put them under a carpet over which we constantly walked. Then, after several weeks of this treatment, the flowers were dry, pressed and ready for making into a flower picture. Over time quite a few beautiful pictures were produced, framed and then given as gifts to various friends who really seem to appreciate them.

The reason we had left Lebanon was that we could no longer educate our two oldest boys in the country as schooling for them had become non-existent. Now in Cyprus, at great cost, our boys were able to attend schools following the English educational system that were for the children of families on the British military base close to where we now lived. This meant that we had a lot of interaction with both military and civilian support people who lived on the base. It just so happened that one of the pictures got into the hands of the headmaster of our boy's school. One day he approached Doreen and invited her to participate in an exhibition of art work produced by people on the base. We felt very privileged as we neither lived on the base nor had any military connection. The exhibition lasted a few days and because the majority of exhibits were paintings the novelty of pressed flower pictures attracted much attention. We were rather taken aback when people wanted to purchase the pictures as we had given such a matter no thought at all. Indeed, at that time, every picture that had been made was designated to be given as a gift to various friends when the exhibition was over.

Local civilians were allowed onto the base to view the exhibition and a few days later a gentleman contacted Doreen and asked if she would exhibit her work in one of the nearby five star hotels that he owned and managed. The hotel would provide and set up the display stands and provide drinks and refreshments for the opening reception to be attended by the mayor and other local dignitaries. The exhibition would last for three days. Everything would be provided at no cost to us and furthermore the hotel did not require any commission from the sale of any pictures that they anticipated would be sold.

Now the Christian charity we were working with, rightfully, had to agree with any income producing work we did and required that any such income went into the organisation's account and not into our own pockets. Our director, an artist himself, readily agreed for Doreen to work on this project. Thus followed many long days and late nights as some seventy pictures were created. The pictures ranged in size from twenty by fifteen centimetres to eighty by fifty centimetres. They were all displayed under non reflective glass in a variety of frames.

When they were made we were faced with the job of pricing them for sale but had no idea of what we should be charging. A few days before the exhibition the pictures were spread out all over our dining room when a friend, who lived the other end of Cyprus, dropped in to visit. When she saw them tears came into her eyes and she exclaimed "These are so beautiful – where are they from, why are they all here?" Explanations followed together with our dilemma concerning pricing them. "Oh, don't worry, I will help you price them. In England I had a florists shop and we used to sell some pictures like these".

The evening opening, ribbon cutting, reception was a truly grand affair attended by many more people than we ever dreamed of coming. A pastor friend we knew from our time in Lebanon gave a short opening speech where he talked about the beauty of God's creation and quoted and spoke about some words of Jesus concerning the "flowers of the field".

"See how the flowers of the field grow. They do not labour or spin. Yet I tell you that not even Solomon in all his splendour was dressed like one of these. If that is how God clothes the grass of the field, which is here today and tomorrow is thrown into the fire, will he not much more clothe you—you of little faith? But seek first his kingdom and his righteousness, and all these things will be given to you as well". *(Matthew 6 v 28-33)*

That evening and the days to follow exceeded all our expectations. That first evening, although they could not be released till the exhibition ended, all the pictures that were up for sale were purchased. We were amazed how a few flowers picked from the hard stony ground led to two exhibitions and the sale of pictures that were to then go to many different countries.

It turned out that the hotel received some good publicity because of the exhibition and this led to another top hotel in the capital wanting Doreen to replicate the event in their hotel. Sadly she had to decline as we were shortly due to leave the island to return to England. But it turned out that the money received from the sale of the pictures went a long way to paying for our air tickets back to England.

As we looked back on all that had transpired we asked ourselves whether a supernatural hand was as work or if we had just witnessed a whole series of helpful coincidents?

40

An Easter Service

"I've arranged an Easter Sunday morning service and I'd like you to preach at it" declared a friend who had just dropped into my office. He then explained that he had persuaded the sceptical owner of a local 5* hotel that it would be good for the hotel's image if they were able to advertise a Christian service to be held on Easter Sunday. So it transpired that the owner manager of the hotel agreed to provide, free of charge, suitable seating in one of the conference rooms. Furthermore he would advertise the service, not only in his own hotel but also in two other big adjacent hotels that at that time were owned by members of his extended family. My friend now had to put together the form of service – the musicians, the hymns and the prayers but at least the preacher was booked. On Easter morning we arrived at the hotel with no idea as to how many might attend the service. It could be that only those due to take part would be there or could our prayers be answered and we would see a good gathering of hotel guests – we had just no idea what to expect. As the advertised commencement time approached people began to flood in and very quickly the conference room was full. When the hotel owner saw what was happening he mobilised his staff who drew back a dividing partition wall in order to double the size of the room. More chairs were set out and we were able to begin the service only a few minutes late with many, many more people attending than we had even dared to hope for.

Then together this one off international congregation joyfully celebrated the resurrection of the Lord Jesus Christ. We were able to declare that Jesus, who died to bring us "back to God from the dark paths of sin", was risen from the dead, was alive and at work in the world today and wanted us to come to Him and serve Him as our risen Saviour and friend.

Talking to the people after the service we found out that although the majority of people were from Europe and the Middle East in fact every continent of the world, except for Antarctica, was represented. We were very surprised when some identified themselves as Muslims while others said they were communists but all said that they had appreciated the experience and it had given them things to think about! Most of the participants were holiday makers who expressed their delight at unexpectedly being able to attend an Easter service in English at the time of Western Easter in a country where Eastern Easter would be celebrated a couple a weeks later.

Now in the "West" we celebrate Christmas day on 25th December but in much of the Middle East the local Orthodox Christian community celebrate Christmas day on 7th January, although Christmas Eve on 6th January plays a significant part in the celebrations. Likewise Western Easter and Eastern Easter, whose dates change every year, are usually celebrated on different days. The reason for the difference is that the Western Church follows the old Julian calendar, while the Orthodox Church uses the Gregorian calendar. This had first hit home to us when on our first Western Christmas morning in Jordan we had woken to the usual noise of traffic and the sight of the children going to school. It was just a normal day.

Our helpful hotel owner was absolutely delighted with the overwhelming response of the hotel guests and insisted that we join him for coffee. To our astonishment he then wanted to pay us but seemed to understand when we told him that it was our privilege to be able to share the good news of Jesus freely with others. He then asked us if we would arrange a carol service in the hotel at Western Christmas time. We assured him that we would be delighted to do so and then and there put a tentative date in the diary.

After that we continued to talk together for a while and were both surprised and delighted when he told us that he was going to give us a free annual pass for our family to use the hotel's sports and swimming pool facilities. The normal cost of such an annual pass at that luxury hotel was well outside our price range and so gladly, with our heart full of praise to God for His provision, we accepted the owner manager's gift.

So it happened that all the years we lived in Cyprus we took an Easter service and a Carol service and carol singing at Christmas in that hotel.

Every year the owner renewed our free pass to use the hotel's sports facilities and our family enjoyed many happy hours spent in and around the swimming pool.

Conclusion

On many occasions in my life people have encouraged me with a verse of scripture found in the book of Proverbs (cpt.3 v 5-6). In the old Kings James translation it reads as follows:

"Trust in the LORD with all thine heart; and lean not unto thine own understanding. In all thy ways acknowledge him, and he shall direct thy paths".

However the paraphrase Message Bible (MSG) gives a certain added clarity to this injunction as it reads as follows:

"Trust GOD from the bottom of your heart: don't try to figure out everything on your own. Listen for GOD's voice in everything you do, everywhere you go; he's the one who will keep you on track. Don't assume that you know it all. Run to GOD! Run from evil".

Throughout our lives together Doreen and I have always sought to trust in the Lord and listen to God's voice. I am the first to admit that I have failed to trust and listen on many occasions but He has always remained true to His promise found in Hebrews (cpt. 13 v 5) that:

"Never will I leave you; never will I forsake you".

I have always held on to that promise of God and He has also indeed directed our paths and kept us on the right track.

The book title **"*It Just So Happened*"** came to us one day when we heard that phrase being used. It reminded us of a song that very much summed up our life journey.

> "I do not know what lies ahead,
>
> the way I cannot see,
>
> yet one stands near to be my guide.
>
> He'll show the way to me.
>
> I know who holds the future,
>
> and He'll guide me with His hand,
>
> with God **things just don't happen**,
>
> everything with Him is planned.
>
> So as I face tomorrow,
>
> with its problems large and small,
>
> I'll trust the God of miracles,
>
> Give to Him my all."

Previously a friend had been talking about *"God Incidents"* in people's lives and the words *Supernatural Incidents* came to mind as part of a working title for the stories I was beginning to write. However when it came to complete the title the decision became much more difficult. What should the second part of the working title be? Should I add *"and Welcome Coincidents"*, *"or Timely Coincidents"*, or *"and / or Timely Coincidents"*. The final decision was that it should be *"and Timely*

Coincidents". Subsequently, however, that working title became the subtitle.

The dilemma concerning the second part of the title arose from the realisation that people would view the stories very differently depending on their belief in a God and the way that they perceive that He is at work in the world today.

As Christians we believe that God is "always present, always knowing and always powerful," or to use three relevant theological terms, God is omnipresent, omniscient and omnipotent. In other words, God knows everything and has the power to do anything. Everything is therefore in His absolute control and consequently coincidents do not occur.

Others would say, while also fully believing those same attributes of God that, He does not micro-manage our lives and furthermore that He encourages us to use our free will to make our own choices in life. We are not robots.

These two seemingly different concepts or views of how God directs our paths would appear to contradict each other but it is obvious that the Bible teaches both concepts. Perhaps my choice of title shows you where I stand!

Then there is a third group of people who do not believe in a God who would say everything in this life is just down to luck and that all the incidents related were just a series of timely coincidents – they just so happened. If this describes you then I trust that the stories will have given you something to consider carefully.

As I came to the end of writing these stories I was reading in the Bible book of Deuteronomy (cpt. 4 v 9) and I found that it explained exactly why I had first put pen to paper (or more accurately fingers to keypad) to produce these short accounts drawn from our life abroad. However when I then turned to the paraphrase of the Living Bible (TLB) I felt that this summed up my thinking and desire even more "accurately".

"But watch out! Be very careful never to forget what you have seen God doing for you. May his miracles have a deep and permanent effect upon your lives! Tell your children and your grandchildren about the glorious miracles he did".

I started out with the expectation of writing just a few short pieces for the benefit of my family but as I wrote many more, temporarily forgotten, instances came to mind. I realised that the many occurrences of the Lord's help and intervention in our affairs had indeed had "*a deep and permanent effect upon your lives!*" After all when God performs a "miracle" in our lives one cannot ever forget it or be unchanged by it.

So, having had time to read, and ponder have you decided which of the stories told were Supernatural Incidents and which were Timely Coincidents used by a loving God for our good?

About the Author

David Holmes was a science teacher by profession with further training in educational TV production. After twelve years teaching science in schools in England both he and his wife Doreen had a definite "call" from God to serve Him in the Middle East. Then followed twelve years working with MECO (Middle East Christian Outreach) where they were pioneers in Christian video in Arabic. On return to England he retrained as a financial adviser and directed his own financial consulting company. However he and his wife remained very active in Christian work, preaching and teaching. Several years after returning to England he became a Trustee / Treasurer of MECO UK and Ireland and helped oversee its merger with SIM (Serving in Mission). Now retired David and Doreen enjoy time spent with their three sons and eight grandchildren in the North of England.

The author can be contacted via email – *itjustsohappened@yahoo.com*